Lisa McDonald IS a genuine thought-leader who definitely walks her talk, and who continues to live her life Fearlessly!

I had the personal honor of reading Lisa's manuscript, and was both captivated and impressed by her courageous, WARRIOR SPIRIT! Lisa is a remarkable example to us all of the profound importance of choosing to relinquish fear and to instead, embrace courage!

I highly recommend this book being added to anyone's reading list - anyone who authentically values personal growth and personal development!

Way to go, Lisa!

— *Patty Aubery, Jack Canfield*
The Canfield Training Group

I am honored to have met Lisa McDonald when she attended The Enlightened Bestseller Mastermind program that I co-led in 2015. At the time, her book *#LivingFearlessly* was in its infancy. It's been inspiring to watch Lisa's journey and to see her important message be shared with the world through this book and through her global radio podcast, which I was delighted to be a guest on. I recommend this book and I support Lisa's mission to help people fear less and live more!

— *Marci Shimoff, #1 New York Times and*
Bestselling author of 'Happy for No Reason'

For quite some time, Lisa McDonald has worked diligently in the pursuit of helping others. She is an exemplary example of the indomitable human spirit. *#LivingFearlessly* will truly help others to help themselves.

— *Dave Pelzer, Author of A Child Called "It" and National Jefferson Award Recipient*

How Lisa survived can only be summed up in one word; resilience.

This is a testament to her strength, and I highly recommend you get an extra copy for anyone who has survived abuse. They will be glad you did."

— *Brad Szollose, Award-Winning Business Author, TEDX Speaker, Former C-Level Executive*

Fear, in one form or another is something that we encounter on a daily basis. *#LivingFearlessly* is where we wish we could live. So how can we find the courage to face the things we fear, the things that block us from our greatness? The answer is; we must find those who on a daily basis face their fears, not because they are without fear, but because they are willing to embrace the courage required to get "it" (the fearful thing) done.

Lisa McDonald is such a person! There might be no better person around who can walk you and I through the potential emotional landmines that block your way.

Lisa's courage, grit, commitment and hustle are an inspiration to many, including me. As you read through the pages of this book you will have a sincere sense that Lisa is by your side, because she will be guiding you to your very best self every step of the way, because that's what she does.

— *Dov Baron: Inc Top 100 Leadership Speaker, Top 30 Global Leadership Guru, Bestselling Author, and Impact Strategist www.FullMontyLeadership.com*

Lisa McDonald has written a must-read primer for anyone who wants to live fearlessly. She gives a firsthand account of how she has overcome her personal challenges, developed and lived her mission to not fear but persist and has become a top podcaster with a message, for you to "Go for it and live your purpose"… Read this book - and learn from one of the best.

— *Dave Sanderson, President Dave Sanderson Speaks International and Survivor of the Miracle on the Hudson*

One cannot rely upon external circumstances for authentically *Living Fearlessly*. The willingness to do so and the required work has to come from within, which Lisa's message so clearly illustrates!

— *Janet Bray Attwood, New York Times Best Selling Author*

There's no one way to prepare for unforeseen circumstances, but being mentally tough can help us get through challenging events – in business and in life. In sharing her personal experiences, author Lisa McDonald gives honest advice on how to overcome life's challenges and free yourself in order to live fearlessly.

— *Jeffrey Hayzlett, Primetime TV & Radio Host, Speaker, Author and Part-Time Cowboy*

Sharing stories empowers others in their own unique journey and Lisa McDonald is taking a true leap of faith by inviting us into her life by keeping it real.

Inspiring, heartfelt and courageous… a must read for anyone on a journey to *#LivingFearlessly*.

— *Trish Tonaj, Author, Coach, Speaker*

I was an instant fan and admirer of Lisa's when we first got on the phone to discuss my upcoming appearance as her guest on her two Global radio/podcast platforms. I am extremely excited!

As our discussion unfolded, I was struck with amazement by Lisa's fierce grit and gumption! Lisa is a woman on an undeniable mission in her quest to uplift others to fear less and to live more!

All of Lisa's bodies of work, messaging, branding, platforms, genuine engagement, and her command of the English language are extraordinary! Lisa is laser focused, resilient. She is a force to be reckoned with, and is without question... Living Fearlessly!

I highly, highly endorse Lisa's latest book, *#LivingFearlessly!*

— *Ben Gay III, "The Closers"*

#LivingFearlessly is a must read book for anyone who finds themselves immobilized by fear and for whatever the reason. As Lisa McDonald consistently says, "If I can choose to live fearlessly with everything I have been through in my life so then can you. It's a choice!" Lisa McDonald's Light is Bright! Her message is a profoundly important one - a message everyone stands to benefit from! It is the gift that keeps on giving!

— *Marshall Goldsmith, two-time Thinkers 50 World's #1 Leadership Thinker.*

Immense courage is what it must have taken Lisa to share her story. Leaving no stone unturned she has peeled back the curtain of her life and allowed us to have a profoundly intimate look into her personal struggles and challenges, marvel at her will to survive and totally understand what fuels her passion and purpose today to Live her life Fearlessly!

— *Jane Blaufus, Bestselling Author, International Speaker, Business Coach*

In *#LivingFearlessly,* Lisa McDonald incredibly and bravely walks the reader through her very own hero's journey, one where she bares her soul like very few could. The book begins with a deep dive into her turmoil and immediately pulls the reader out to demonstrate how precisely she went inward, expertly dissected her own internal dialogue to learn at an early age to befriend herself and to share with us how we should all treat ourselves with the utmost compassion, no matter our situation. Lisa tells a heart wrenching story of how she overcame and we get a glimpse of the unbelievable strength inside this powerhouse of a woman who is now living life with the purpose to help others! This is the extraordinary account of a truly beautiful and courageous woman. In her triumph, she lights the way for us to triumph as well.

— *Zahra Karsan, PMP, NLP Founder & CEO, Get ZENd*

Lisa McDonald is the most iconic person you will know. She gives of herself nobly, helping others to live fearlessly and embrace where they are in life and to never give up. She tackles a range of obstacles we all have in our life, including those less 'fun' or popular. Lisa not only tells a story of personal development, she is living proof we can all live fearlessly. Lisa is the very essence of overcoming personal challenges and serving others both personally and professionally. Who doesn't want to be a better person?

— *Connie Pheiff, Chair & CEO, Pheiff Group, Inc.*

Lisa McDonald is a force to be reckoned with. Lisa's relentless drive, and ability to motivate others to live a life of being Fearless, is second to none. Lisa is a cheerleader for anyone and everyone who chooses to live an empowered life. Her book shares her own raw journey of previously living in fear to becoming a person who now only lives and teaches living fearlessly. Her global radio show/podcast is always thought provoking, entertaining, and inspirational. Lisa's book will not only offer you a fresh new perspective but it will equally inspire you to Live Fearlessly!

In Service to Your Success!

— Cameron Steele, Co-Owner of Contact Talk Radio Network,
Clear Conscious Media LFP

I'm a big fan of Lisa McDonald and her vital message of Living Fearlessly. As the host of Reinvention Radio, I am particularly drawn to each of my guests' personal plights. Lisa clearly personifies reinvention and has illustrated hers in powerful fashion within the pages of her book, #LivingFearlessly!

Her courage, vulnerability, and candidness demonstrate for all of us that it is possible to live a life absent of fear! I highly recommend it.

— Steve Olsher - NY Times bestselling author of What Is Your WHAT?
Discover The ONE Amazing Thing You Were Born To Do and host of
Reinvention Radio

It is an honor to have the opportunity to read the incredible story of Lisa. She has given us the story of her life in detail and how she was able to maintain her positive outlook and personality. One passage sums up not only her life story, but the same can be said to each of us who follow her example.

The passage reads, "Like everything else in my life that I may not have understood or received adequate closure on, I have instead, as cited throughout the entirety of my book, chosen to focus on the gifts, the lessons, the ways in which I can turn darkness into brightness and not only for myself but for the collective. I believe this is my purpose. I believe this to be my personal Universal-Calling in life."

We can all learn from Lisa's lesson. Believe in your purpose and turn your darkness into brightness.

— David L. Brown, Business Plan Answer Man

Looking for permission to embrace your greatness? In *#LivingFearlessly* author Lisa McDonald shares her own personal journey to recognizing her worth and shares how all of us can do the same. No matter where you're from or what you've endured, Lisa's story is sure to give you the motivation to press forward towards your destiny.

— Cyrus Webb, Media Personality/Author/Top 300 Amazon.com Reviewer

Lisa's story is riveting. She shares her journey and what it takes to not allow pain to define you. Becoming a thriver is a choice and Lisa is a role model for anyone who has endured pain as a child. This book is a great resource for anyone who wants to regain power and create a fulfilling life.

— Roxanne Derhodge MSC., Registered Psychotherapist,
Author and Keynote Speaker

In her book, Lisa shares her riveting and courageous journey outlining her numerous crucibles. Lisa is determined not to be defined by them instead to thrive because of them.

— *Linda Marshall, President at Marshall Connects Inc.*
Author, Television Host, Motivational Speaker, EQ Facilitator

Lisa opens her soul to share her personal crucible and the process of reframing negative events to build her own positive framework to support moving forward with resilience, compassion and persistence. Lisa rewrites her past to create a better future for her kids.

— *James Kelley, Ph.D., author of The Crucible's Gift: 5 Lessons from*
Authentic Leaders Who Thrive in Adversity, speaker and leadership expert.

How does a child survive the ultimate betrayal, yet grow up to be a thriving, joy-filled adult? In Lisa McDonald's *#LivingFearlessly*, I found myself sitting on the edge of my seat crying, filled with rage, and compassion, as the author exposes the years of devastating sexual abuse, angst and frustration, and eventual redemption. This is the most powerful book I have ever read, and it took me on an emotional rollercoaster.

Lisa McDonald embodies the crux of her message, living fearlessly, wholeheartedly. She is funny, authentic, raw, and full of talent. I love her message and can't wait to read more of her work in the future.

— *Serena Dyer, Daughter of Dr. Wayne Dyer*

I had the pleasure of appearing as a former guest on *Living Fearlessly* with Lisa McDonald - Lisa's global weekly radio and podcast show. Being connected to Lisa on social media and as someone who is heavily entrenched in the book and branding world; watching the evolution of Lisa's *#LivingFearlessly* journey blossom and explode into what it has now become... has been truly remarkable!

Lisa very successfully navigates and maximizes all of her various platforms for the obvious purpose of imparting her message with the collective - uplifting people to fear less and to live more.

Lisa's commitment to empowering others to empower themselves is very inspiring. I have no doubt Lisa's book will connect and resonate with thousands of others outside of the generous following she has organically already cultivated for herself.

Your message is a powerfully important one, Lisa! To your continued success!

— *Rick Frishman, Bestselling Author, Publisher &*
Speaker Rickfrishman.com

#LIVINGFEARLESSLY
WITH LISA MCDONALD

UPLIFTING YOU TO FEAR LESS AND TO LIVE MORE!

LISA MCDONALD

Motivational PRESS®
LEADERS IN GLOBAL PUBLISHING

Published by Motivational Press, Inc.
1777 Aurora Road
Melbourne, Florida, 32935
www.MotivationalPress.com

Manufactured in the United States of America.

ISBN: 978-1-62865-586-5

CONTENTS

ACKNOWLEDGEMENTS

I am immensely grateful to all the people in my life who have shown up as mirrors, teachers, mentors, and leaders.

Thank you to Oprah Winfrey and Dave Pelzer, who unbeknownst to them at the time...were profoundly instrumental to my inner journey of reclaiming 'self.'

To my two beautiful children, Quinn and Olivia, who are my everything! Eternal love and gratitude to both of you for uplifting me to fear less and to live more in the here and now!

Chapter 1

I NEED A VACATION FROM MY VACATION

"I am thirsty," I said – looking up to the white-haired man I called Grandpa. The two of us were nestled beside one another on what was to be my bed for the duration of my family vacation in the UK.

"I have something for you to drink," Grandpa responded with, as excited fingers began to unzip his trousers. As he arched his back to maneuver the loosening of his underwear, I saw for the first time what I later came to understand, was a man's full erection. I was four years old.

I remember confusingly watching him as he stroked himself with his right hand. I remember being astutely aware of a facial expression I had never before recognized – a glazed over, out-of-your-body, euphoric look. I remember hearing un-familiar sounds escape his mouth. I remember Grandpa clutching the back of my head and navigating my mouth to his penis, while assuring me that my drink was well on its way.

After what felt eternal to me within that span of time – sure enough – something I had never before tasted – squirted down the back of my throat. He coaxed me to swallow so as to satiate my thirst. "That's a good girl, Lisa," spewed his proud; approving voice. I watched him quickly dress himself and descend down the stairs where the other adults, including my parents, were congregated. I heard faint laughter and joke-telling simultaneous to hearing my own silent tears bounce off my cheek; hitting the soon to be completely saturated pillow.

On whatever day it was into this hellish nightmare of a so-called vacation, I cringed when Grandpa had received permission to take lucky ol' me – not my brother – for quality one-on-one time to visit the shops of South Ockendon, Essex, England. The exchange for my complicit silence was candy, a Snoopy Watch, and my first pair of children's slightly high-heeled shoes – decorated in red fabric with a flower patterned design.

After being pampered with gifts and tokens – I remember the two of us venturing off the beaten path – hand-in-hand. For any onlookers, it must have appeared as a postcard special, sweet grandfather and grand-daughter moment whilst passing us by; going in the opposite direction. Eventually, the traffic, the tourists, the town-folk and anyone else with a face or presence, began to disappear from where I was being led.

I remember being in the middle of a plush green, barren field, covered in moss and ivy and to the right of us – was a tall, iron-rod fence, separating him and me on one side, and older men adorned in hospital attire, on the other side.

Grandpa Reg stood to the left of me – nose to nose with the fence. It wasn't simply curiosity, which drew these men dressed in hospital garb – closer to us – it was as if Reg and these (mentally-ill) patients – conversed in their own energetic and telepathic language. Almost on cue – Grandpa dropped his trousers once again, while a couple of the others who were directly facing us – began doing to themselves, what I had only ever witnessed once before and on the night of my wanting a drink.

I was eye-level with all these men's genitalia and the hand that had clasped mine – the one which brought me to this scary, strange, foreign place – was the same hand now guiding mine toward my Grandpa's once again, very swollen penis.

When all was said and done, Grandpa and I reversed course back to the house, while the focus then quickly shifted to how lovely my new shoes were and how spectacular it was that the hands on my new Snoopy watch were tennis rackets – chasing the green tennis balls second-hand. This was a very much-welcomed distraction for both of us even if veiled in emotional manipulation.

I remember at a very young age, being cognizant of what it was to know the outside world, gleaning a vastly different Lisa from the Lisa I knew on the inside. This dual-reality was proven in the certificate awards I had received at Girl Guide Camp and Canterbury Hills Camp, where I was acknowledged and recognized for having the 'Happiest Smile.' Of course I had the Happiest Smile, I had been conditioned and groomed to keep it plastered upon my face so as to never alert anyone of the vile truth…the truth that kept my spirit submerged in less than happy waters.

LIVING FEARLESSLY DOWNLOAD

I learnt at a very young age and as a result of what you have just read in the aforementioned, the imperativeness of internal SELF-DIALOGUE. I was the only one (as far as I knew) who knew what was happening to me. On a good day and without challenge – we are often times alone with our innermost thoughts. On a difficult day under extreme challenge – we are also alone with our innermost thoughts. To survive what I had endured without having a complete mental collapse, I unconsciously knew I had to embrace and protect myself as lovingly as possible from the inside. I knew I had to talk to myself almost as if a separate person, who befriends, comforts and consoles another individual faced with crisis. I learnt how to master the life-skill and coping mechanism of how to intervene by talking myself down and talking myself through whatever I encountered. For as many times as I found myself being in the same unfortunate situation of requiring constructively positive, SELF-DIALOGUE – what I was also inadvertently accomplishing by doing so, was strengthening and developing a very important muscle – my mental muscle – aka – my MINDSET - for everything else which lied ahead of me – equally requiring me to kindly and lovingly dialogue with myself. As despicable as these acts perpetrated against me were, it actually propelled me into becoming a very intrinsically, emotionally strong individual, which further prepared me for many unforeseen future challenges, where I would on many occasions, need to lean on myself for sole support and guidance, hence being my best friend and talking to myself as such in order to RISE. There is always brightness, which is birthed out of darkness. IT IS A CHOICE!

CHAPTER 2

MY RE-BIRTH

June 27, 2014 – 10:30pm

"Hello, Lisa. This is Tom (my step-father). I wanted to let you know that at 8:30pm this evening, your Mum passed away in hospice, and while in one of her last most lucid moments, she asked me to promise her to relay a message to you. She asked me to tell you that she forgives you and that she has also asked Jesus Christ to forgive you."

After less than twenty-four hours of learning that my mum passed on due to metastatic breast cancer, and after processing that she had been admitted into hospice weeks prior to her passing, and knowing that no one shared this with me (at her request) – I was awestruck with a moment of full-circle revelation and clarity. In realizing that I was not invited to attend her service, I also began to accept the cold reality that my mum consciously opted for her last parting words to me (knowing there would be no closure, recourse, or follow up discussion between the two of us) to be words and sentiments not indicative of love or self-reflection or even volunteered apology to me, but rather, her last, carefully selected message to be relayed to me, was one she potentially chanced leaving a permanent indelible mark on my soul.

Fortunately and thankfully, her parting message, indirectly to be shared with me, was in fact, the greatest gift she ever gave me, outside of life itself. My Mum's 'death' signified and truly spawned my re-birth.

It took my becoming a mother myself to deeply connect the dots on the realization of not only how fragmented and splintered my relationship with my Mum had always been, but also too, how the extreme polarities existent in our roles and identities as women, as human beings, and as mothers – were glaringly magnified.

How my Mum chose to go out on her deathbed – with her imparted last words, intended for me to learn, and only after she had passed over – was the lingering, devastating, spiritual and soulful slaughter she wished to gift me with. As had been true in the tangible sense – Mum always had to have the last word, whether it was timed with her kicking me off her turf or when she was bailing from mine. The door was to be permanently slammed in my face without any prospect of re-establishing any form of true, meaningful, genuine, healthy or reciprocal closure.

My heartfelt assessment and evaluation of this third-party message – intended from a mother to her daughter – the first-born child – instinctively resonated with my own maternal instinct. I dug deep – plunged into the mother spirit and tried to envision myself on my own deathbed – questioning what, if anything, would be my last words of choice to be communicated from my heart and soul to my child – and regardless of estrangement – regardless of having shared a tumultuous, on and off relationship, throughout the course of my own journey with motherhood. Knowing my words would be definitively spoken – never to be afforded the opportunity for retraction, elaboration, nor could I know to the degree my words would potentially penetrate or sear the psyche, heart or soul of my child – my child who would learn of my last words and maternal message, while also trying to grapple with the uncertainty and painful task of attempting to grieve a death in a non-typical fashion, on top of my child being a single-parent mother herself to two young children and knowing firsthand the ongoing challenges that feat alone represents for anyone faced with such a daily struggle – a predicament my Mum had firsthand knowledge, understanding, insight and experience with herself.

Could I ever voluntarily impose such colossal carnage on my children, while on my deathbed? After reaching an instantaneous, internal, maternal answer of a resounding 'NO' – it was in fact in that precise moment – that the emotional shackles loosened – it was in that exact moment that more than forty years of on/off dead weight dissolved and began to evaporate. It was in that finite, transformational moment that I was re-born. Unbeknownst to my Mum, she had given birth to me twice. Her death manifested what I can only now say with authentic, heart-held conviction that the clarity I had once before lacked – in the knowing of my true life's purpose – to embark upon the journey of LIVING FEARLESSLY myself and to reach the masses with my message, had unleashed! My Mum's so-called END if you will was the MOTHER of all my BEGINNINGS.

Aside from the birthing of my own two beautiful children – THIS… was the core foundational beginning of Lisa McDonald, choosing to embrace and reclaim her life of Living Fearlessly!

LIVING FEARLESSLY DOWNLOAD

The old adage, 'We are born alone and we die alone,' strongly resonates with me, particularly when we all experience life, sharing the same spectrum of emotions. No matter how unique our individual journey, no matter how different our individual circumstances in life may be – none of us are immune from knowing what it is to feel pain, to feel challenged, to feel alone, to feel un-liked and un-loved, to feel isolated, to feel invisible, to feel misunderstood, misrepresented, to feel unheard and invalidated. We know for a fact that for all the statistics floating around in the world, all the necessary support groups, crisis hotlines, programs, workshops, counselors, therapists, social services, self-help books and the list goes on – we know that for whatever we have struggled with in our own lives, we remember how we felt even if how we felt was numb. I believe people who have been exposed to pain and darkness the most, tend to be the people who are most inclined to develop their compassion and empathy muscle for others. When one has travelled to the abyss, and knows what it feels like to be on the outside – outside of happiness, personal safety, love, respect, ourselves, and of anything our souls require for nurturance, for sustenance and for growth – we know it is not a sphere of existence we would wish upon anyone, therefore, for those of us who have been submerged in the darkness – we are not only the first ones to recognize and detect it in others, but we are also the first responders in coming to other people's aid because we have developed the compassion and empathy muscle. Again, it is a CHOICE as to which path you choose to travel down. Do you become bitter, jaded, self-absorbed, disconnected or rather, do you find the brightness within the darkness and in-turn, decide to pay-it-forward and be-of-service-to-others, knowing that we are all in this together? IT IS A CHOICE!

Chapter 3

BLOWING OUT SOMEONE ELSE'S CANDLE

As my Mum blew out the candles on her birthday cake – I secretly; energetically emitted my own wish into the Universe. My Wish: 'Please get his hand out of my crotch. Please make him stop touching me while everyone else is singing Happy Birthday.'

This was to be the MOTHER of all summers – the one which changed the course of future direction for my family – my family now all congregated around a rectangular table - long table cloth draped over everyone's laps – the summer my Mum was to impart the news to her Mum and step-father, Reg – that she and my Dad were on the cusp of separating with the intent to divorce and unbeknownst to me at the time – the same summer my ongoing years of sexual abuse was to be 'disclosed.'

As I always did when I was being abused – I would seek refuge in the four corners of the ceiling (if indoors – the sky, if outdoors). My spirit would float above, and from a bird's eye view – the self-protector version of Lisa, would coach me through the scenario. I was socially cued and reminded to adorn the permanent smile upon my face so as not to tip-off the world to the reality of what was, once again, unfolding in front of everyone and usually while underneath the same roof as those whose inherent role it was - to be my actual protectors.

I distinctly remember thinking to myself – how incredibly ballsy it was of my 'Grandpa' to risk his hand navigating its way to my private region, while elbow to elbow at a table full of family members – all of whom were there to celebrate his step-daughter's birthday. As discreetly as I could, my hand met his underneath the tablecloth and I pinched the hell out of his skin, as hard as I could to thwart off his advances and I didn't care if he winced or gasped or cried out. He would not relent nor would I. Finally, I gouged him so hard it resulted in his wine spilling – toppling from his weaker hand. In the rush to sponge up the mess and ensure his glass was once again, filled – I quietly declared a personal victory not to mention a wee bit of a reprieve.

Upon arriving home from my Mum's birthday party at her best friend's house – I quietly escaped to my bedroom; closing the door behind me and laid down on my bed; eyes fixated on the ceiling – lost in my own thoughts of just wanting to forever disappear – pleading for this summer to hurry up and be over – for my 'Grandpa' to already be back in England. Being cognizant of time, I also knew that to rush time and to wish for these things, was also to conversely quicken the pace of my Mum and Dad's impending plans to officially part ways – something no child ever wishes for no matter how dysfunctional the dynamics.

Caught up in the contemplation and pondering of all these dual realities of my life – my Mum broke my thought processes by entering my room and sitting down beside me on my bed. Looking down upon my face, she proceeded to ask me a plethora of questions as to why I was so quiet and withdrawn. She went through the laundry list of asking if I was upset with her, my Dad, or my brother. I continued to fire off the robotic response of 'NO' until, something profound spewed from her mouth – so much so that I made a mental note to revisit what she said at a later time. My Mum had cautiously and apprehensively asked me if, "HE did something to me."

Immediately, every fiber of my being shifted – the hairs on my arms stood up. My Mum initiated the asking of this question with a distinct sense of knowingness and she had asked the question without referring to 'HIM' by name – Reg to her or Grandpa to me. This was my first glimpse into what I could realistically and chronologically understand at that time of intuitively sensing that my Mum had some inclination of what, 'HE' was all about – perhaps, her knowing to some degree and on some level what he had in fact been perpetrating on me.

The floodgates of inner questions poured through me – "Why would she ask me that?" "Why would she ask me in such a way so as to suggest a lack of surprise or ultimate shock on her part?" The defining moment of what this significant pivotal exchange shared between us – did not fully compute for me in that exact moment, however; intuitively, I knew something was 'off.'

LIVING FEARLESSLY DOWNLOAD

In addition to honing my internal SELF-DIALOGUE (muscle) becoming my best friend (muscle) number one protector (muscle) albeit an unfair age to have to hone these skills, nevertheless, they are still beneficial life-skills-tack on to the ever-growing list – INTUITION (muscle). Regardless of the circumstances, which forced me to have to tap into my inner-resources; my inner-reserve, I could not be more grateful to not only have an authentically healthy and solid core sense of self, but what a gift to have had enough practice and opportunity for insight, to trust my own intuition. Regardless of the circumstances for which these skills derived out of, they have assisted me time and time again and have helped me alleviate and avert in some cases, my accumulating unnecessary additional pain and struggle. INTUITION and choosing to trust my intuition, has helped keep me safe as an adult. Intuition and choosing to trust my intuition has helped me make many spectacular decisions in my life – has allowed me to give myself permission to take smart risks and prevent me from making harmful, unwise ones. This is not to suggest that everything has always worked out for me without mishap or hiccup, rather this is only to say that the mishaps and the hiccups in my life have been more likely to occur when I have chosen to ignore or quell my own intuition. I believe my set of circumstances (sexual abuse) being the type that is synonymous with one being most likely to keep hidden in silence. This is what forced me to go inward as a human being. The concept of one going inward has become all-the-new-rave within personal development. I believe in this whole-heartedly – if we do not spend time with ourselves, or are still with ourselves, or question ourselves, or begin to know and explore ourselves at the deepest core level, how does one authentically begin to grow and flourish as a human being? How does one begin to know?

What they want out of life or trust in what their purpose is, know what their passions are? Know how to fully maximize and optimize this gift of life? How can we be of true, healthy service to others if we question our own sense of self-awareness or are still operating from a place of lack with respect to self-love? If the things that happened to me in my life had not happened to me in my life, would I even care to ponder these deeper, more meaningful expansive type questions? Would I care to be a better person every single day? Would advocating and empowering others, even be on my daily radar? Who knows – perhaps, not. I am grateful that because of the life lessons learned from my experiences, I care to reach other people – connect with other people no matter what they are struggling with, which might be similar or completely different than what I have gone through in my life – the point being, I want to use what has happened to me and my acquired insights gifted to me from healing, mentorship, and personal development, and do my part to contribute toward being part of the collective solution as opposed to part of the ongoing, systemic, inter-generational, problem. IT IS A CHOICE!

CHAPTER 4

CHRISTMAS MEETS TWILIGHT ZONE

Poor personal decisions, lack of guidance, a slew of unresolved issues, and a desperate need for something…someone…anything – led me to being kicked out of high-school and that official notice having arrived at the second parental home, which I no longer lived at. Notice arrived weeks after I had stopped showing up, altogether.

I returned to the town of Dundas, Ontario, Canada, where I had grown up and spent many a year, before setting out to live here, there and everywhere, with a developed pattern of not being able to hold onto a fixed address for any length of significant time. I took up full-time employment at a local health-food store.

During a back-on-again period of communication – I had received the telephone call from my Mum, whom at this time, lived in Raleigh, North Carolina. I had been invited to spend Christmas with her, my brother (who was now living in the states, himself) and my Grandma from England.

Given that my Grandma was in her second marriage (with Reg) and it being taboo of her generation to be a divorced woman, let alone remarried for a second time, and especially given her husband Reg was known as a sexual abuser/pedophile – it was not uncommon for her to travel without him.

I hummed and hawed about whether or not I should go as my Mum and I had not long beforehand; sat in a six-year period of estrangement. For my own healing purposes and emotional sanity – the estrangement would have remained indefinite, however; that all changed immediately when I had received the telephone call from my brother, disclosing that my Mum had been diagnosed with stage 3, breast cancer at 44 years of age. I had reached out to her after all those consecutive years of sheer silence – given that the cancer was in fact said to be quite aggressive and not knowing how long she may have to live. I, for her (own) benefit, peace of mind and for any consumed guilt she may have been harboring – I wanted her to crossover – feeling absolved.

It was with deep angst and with others cautioning me about the potential repercussions I may emotionally and spiritually endure, should I decide to re-open my long-withstanding wound with my Mum that I begrudgingly said yes to her Christmas Holiday invitation. The invitation unfortunately did not come without the guilt-trip being hurled at me when my Mum initially sensed my indecisiveness and uncertainty. I was met with, "Your Grandma isn't getting any younger," "Working at a Health Food store will never afford you the monies to visit her in England on your own dime." And so it continued the onslaught of emotional manipulative tactics I was all too familiar with, which ensued, until I simply decided to concede.

Upon my arrival at the airport, my nerves were completely shot and more so when I locked eyes with the mirror image of myself looking back at me. I could visibly see the changes to my Mum – not only because of six years of estrangement and what that length of time can do to change the appearance of someone, but because she was now adorning a wig and undergoing cancer treatments. I observed six years of aging, in a still very much youthful looking face, although noticing the visible tiredness in her eyes – the same eyes that reciprocated in the once-over examination of me.

To her, I am sure I appeared too thin – unusually pale, even for the wintery washed-out season. I had been doing more than my fair share of drugs at that particular point in my life – fortunately not taking me down a path of addiction, but admittedly, my poor choices were taking me down the rabbit-hole of artificial escapism.

The initial embrace was wrought with immense bitter-sweetness. For me, it felt awkward, yet equally comforting, familiar, but foreign and natural, yet contrived. Simultaneously automatic and robotic – too short and too long in duration. Everything about the relationship was mired in contradictions – even perceivably the simplest of aspects were, often times, overflowing with complexities. The external packaging of us – resembled two peas in a pod, and yet, the inner-wirings of who we individually were, at the core of our own foundations; could not have been more un-recognizable to the third eye.

After the already emotionally heightened greetings at the airport – I was then told by my Mum and stepfather, that we were going to have a discussion at a restaurant before heading to their house. Immediately, my anxiety sky-rocketed through the roof, but who was I to argue, to question or to protest – I was now on their turf, and so, I continued to quell my inner-angst, and simply followed their cue. I had ordered a small appetizer just to be polite and cordial and then, I was blind-sighted by the announcement that instantly propelled my inner-child, floating back up to the four corners of the ceiling – eye-balling me from above.

"We wanted to tell you before taking you back to the house, Lisa – that not only are your brother and Grandma spending Christmas with us this year, but Reg is, too. We want you to know that he is different now. We do not excuse what he has done to you in the past, however, we want you to know that he is on medications to suppress his sexual urges and tendencies – that he has undergone psychotherapy, and we have chosen to forgive him and start over as a family. We do not believe you have anything to worry about, but just to border on caution; we will ensure that you are never left alone in the same room with him, and we will all keep an eye on you during your stay with us."

To say that I was stunned, hurt, triggered, speechless, would be a complete understatement. Those old feelings of abandonment, un-protectiveness and deeply entrenched betrayal all resurfaced with a vengeance for yet the umpteenth time. To date, this will always remain as one of the top surreal moments in the reflecting back upon my life. This bombshell was then followed with the question, "Do you want any dessert before we pay the bill?"

I could not compute on any level what was unfolding here, in front of me. To say I was in the twilight zone, would not even begin to describe the undercurrent of dysfunction and disconnect I had been tossed back into. All my bodily senses failed me – I could not hear, I could not smell, could not taste, could not see, could not speak – everything went static on me. To this day, I am uncertain if in those few moments of complete blankness and nothingness – if it was some form of divine intervention that turned my switch off – installing some type of internal super-power download before switching me back on so as to mechanically navigate me through this Merry Christmas.

I was extremely eased when I saw my brother Craig's face – confused when I made initial eye contact with my Grandma, and immediately repulsed by the ugly elephant in the room, when I had to look at Reg for the first time after so many years. Never did I think I would ever be in his presence again in my lifetime and certainly not on my own volition. While I tried emotionally acclimatizing, once again, to the time warp of dysfunctional 'family' reunification time – I was very astutely aware of how instantaneously everyone immediately fell back into their customary roles of pretending everything was normal – the all-too familiar superficialities, clicked in as if turning on the lights on the Christmas Tree – also automated the reset button on their body language – their simplistic verbal exchanges – each nuance was seemingly contrived and 'safe' in its approach and delivery. The only thing real in the entire house was the artificial tree. The only brightness that shone through was from the decorative lights.

I remember staring at the presents all evenly dispersed underneath the tree and feeling envious of objects that had no feelings. Jealous that such a thing as a Christmas present, could be majestically and pristinely wrapped and that its inside contents could congruently be just as beautiful – that the outside of anything could match its inside, even if it were only a 'thing.' I desperately wanted to be that 'thing' – anything whereby the outside and the inside, complemented one another and could generate some element of joy – even if only temporary and fleeting.

I wanted someone one day to delicately un-wrap the gift of me and love what they discovered on the inside. I wanted one day for me to be able to do the same – and as quickly as I thought these thoughts and wished these wishes – my drifted spirit abruptly returned to the idle chit chat in the kitchen – the opening and closing of oven and fridge doors – the repetitive sounds and movements of people concentrating all their energies on the orchestration of preparing the perfect meal, paralleled with the intentional avoidance of the rapid deterioration of this on-looker in the adjoining room, named Lisa.

The only one out of them all, who predictably kept their protective eye out for me, was of course my brother, Craig. Although, he had not partook in the gong-show conversation at the restaurant, nor was he the one to initiate the scripted conversation of offering lip-service promises and false assurances of my safety or sense of safety, being upheld and considered paramount – it was as always, Craig, who instinctively just knew how to inherently step-in and step-up.

I was immensely grateful to Craig when he joined me on the couch, leaving the others to hover around one another in the kitchen – them being more 'PROTECTIVE' of food not burning, while they diligently conversed in their trivial conversations of 'APPROPRIATE' temperatures and whose 'ROLE' and 'RESPONSIBILITY' it was to 'OVERSEE' what. Everything I witnessed and overheard could only translate for me as a metaphor or an analogy to contrast the ironies and the inequities for what took precedence and priority in any and all given situations, conversations, and circumstance.

I was consistently awestruck by the concerted effort made by all parties, to preserve and maintain at all costs – this ridiculously insulting façade. Not one of them (other than Craig, of course) dared to ask me the question of, 'How Was I?' No, this would bring into focus the reality of how I must truly be fairing and that was too dangerous of terrain to embark upon. Everyone opted to play it safe with the questions, "Are you hungry, Lisa?" "Can I make you a cup of tea?" "Can I get you anything?" To this day, I am challenged by superficial conversation, especially when it is used as an avoidance tactic or to divert personal accountability or to negate individual ownership. I equally struggle with people who elect to play it safe (which for me – is synonymous with playing small) – those who choose to hide behind the veil of perfection – who still perhaps, view vulnerability, candidness, rawness, open-disclosure and full-transparency, as indicators of weakness or 'too much information' – the NIMBY mindset. The people, who live their lives pretending that if something does not exist – then in actuality, it does not and will therefore, simply disappear altogether. The people who are paralyzed to display emotion – who would rather evaporate or implode, than publicly cry – people who cringe or turn the channel on the atrocities of other peoples devastation or crises, otherwise known as their personal hell or life story. People who close the curtains on emotional intelligence – who lock the doors when they get a whiff of those who are fiercely committed to honing their self-awareness – whose DNA consists of jargon, such as personal awareness and personal development.

I have immense compassion for all humans, including those I am not necessarily spiritually aligned with on a deeper, substantive level. I remain steadfast in my compassion for the collective, even though, I admittedly believe that this alternative mindset of some – contributes to the overall complicities of what I deem to be the downfall of our humanity. I am compelled and wired to be an agent of change – to help people make the internal shift – to get off the fence in their own life, which keeps them immobilized by fear – stuck in their complacency and mediocrity. As part of my own journey, I believe I am here to help deconstruct and deprogram those who continue to get in their own way – who elect to buy into the false beliefs and concepts, which only serves to feed their limiting beliefs and erode their most authentic sense of self – who they ultimately were before society, family, and eventually themselves – convinced them of who they should be – what to think and what to believe and who to become. I believe that to remain entrenched in this type of indoctrination is to truly fall short of LIVING and BEING and these two key core-life concepts being central to what I believe to be our BIRTHRIGHT. It is NEVER too late to re-embrace, to re-discover our childlike spirit – the spirit where we are our most curious, adventurous, wondrous, trusting, joy-filled, loving, kind, and passionate about LIFE!

While sprawled out on the couch, enjoying the company and positive distraction of my brother Craig – I was once again reminded of my surroundings, when Reg who exited the kitchen, taking an immediate right-hand turn to ascend the staircase, which led to the upstairs bedrooms – looked down at both Craig and I sitting on the couch and while mid-way up the stairs, looked directly at me – nodded his head sideways; gesturing for me to follow him upstairs. Craig who was very well aware of the strain and lunacy of this entire family dynamic – motioned to jump off the couch – instantly, propelled into brotherly protective mode and at the precise timing of me springing into strategic-offensive positioning. "Craig, please leave it alone. You know I will somehow get blamed for ruining everyone else's Christmas if anything gets said. I have dealt with this for years in silence – I can get through the holidays easier if we just keep this to ourselves." It was clear that Craig felt conflicted by the situation, but being fully aware of our family dynamics to have always been exactly what they were – he begrudgingly conceded by graciously allowing me to dodge another potential landmine.

Slowly and painfully fast forward to the arrival of December 25th – the sole purpose for this celebratory gathering. I have very little recollection of my birthday, four days prior on the 21st, and have almost no recollection of Christmas morning itself, with the customary tradition of taking turns exchanging and opening gifts with one another. However, what I do unfortunately remember and will never forget, and what to this day remains a standout snapshot, defining moment within my ongoing journey of perpetual healing and survival throughout the course of my earlier, fractured self – are the events that unfolded on the eve of December 25th.

We were all beckoned to take our seats at the festively decorated dinner table – cutlery and plate settings perfectly situated in proper, upper-class, British fashion. The only detail out of place and off-center, were the people themselves who the table was set for. As much as I was full of dread to make my way to the table, I was also cognizant of wanting to quickly make my way to the empty seat, situated right beside my brother. As quickly as I plopped myself down in the chair – and almost on calculated cue – I was told by my Mum, that that was not my seat; that there was an actual seating arrangement put in place and I was to change spots with my Grandma. My heart instantly began pounding in my throat and I went back to the four corners of the ceiling. I could not believe – could not fathom – had zero comprehension, how in-spite of how screwed up my relationships history was with my Mum – how asinine this entire sham of a holiday family get-together this visit was, nor could I compute the deceptively manipulative tactics deployed to even have me under the same roof with this man, all these years later – HOWEVER, to configure the seating arrangements in such a way that I was purposely placed right beside him – knowing the last incident I had endured being assaulted, had been beside him at a table for my Mum's birthday all those years beforehand, was simply twisted and deranged for lack of a better description. I could not believe the blatant disconnect that was exponentially unraveling before my very eyes. This was a newly set record for all-time emotional cruelty. I could not wrap my brain around the non-existent maternal or parental instinctiveness to protect one's own flesh and blood – could not make heads or tails of the depths of this type of denial, betrayal, and the dismissiveness – the neglect.

I did not know what was worse in that moment; the fate of this seating arrangement – HIM for the sick pervert he still was and always had been since my earliest childhood recollections or HER – my so-called, MUM – who had delved to a new sub-standard level of having less than zero regard for me as a human being – a child – her child regardless of my then older age. This woman who carried me in her womb for nine months and who gave birth to me.

With my body's weight (which I could not feel), I pushed back my chair – held it open for my Grandma to replace myself in its spot and then sickeningly inched my way closer to the empty chair awaiting me right beside, Reg. Talk about déjà vu! I was once again, precisely to the right of him at another table; celebrating yet, another 'festive' occasion. I have no recollection of how much time had lapsed before my Mum erupted into a fit of rage, and all of it solely directed toward me. Her words of anger were like smelling salts, bringing me back to the here and now – this realm of static-y nothingness I would vacillate in and out of. While, momentarily fumbling to get my mental bearings straight – I 'awoke' to all I can describe as a complete annihilation of what was left of my already dwindling spirit. I was literally hanging by a rapidly fraying thread.

The ambush opener was, "Ever since you've gotten off the plane, you have been nothing but miserable and ungrateful. We flew you here on our dime – gave you an opportunity to see your Grandmother and brother, which you would not have been able to afford on your own. We've spoilt you with lovely Christmas and birthday presents – have tried to show you a good time since you've arrived – taking you here – taking you there – treating you to everything – not asking you to contribute or even lift a finger around the house. We prepared you this beautiful meal on what is supposed to be a special day – a special occasion – one we have not celebrated in many years together as a family. You sit here completely un-communicative and unresponsive – not making any effort or attempt to eat any of what was cooked all-day for you. Your attitude and silence has made everyone uncomfortable and unable to fully enjoy and appreciate what this holiday was intended to be not only for you, but also for everyone else. Once again, you are behaving selfishly and only thinking of yourself. Thanks for ruining my Christmas, Lisa, and probably everyone else's, too."

By this point, it was just she and I at the table. Everyone else had disappeared and left the two of us, alone to once again do battle. Aside from the nano-second moment of feeling as though I had been completely sucker-punched with a velocity of pressure never before been blasted my way – an instant surge of superhero intensity kicked in and seemingly overpowered everything in the room – me, her. I instantly felt as though I had morphed into being ten feet tall – everything outside of me had immediately shrunk in size and dimension in proportion to me. An unexpected strength and power overtook me – invaded my body, my mind and inevitably – my mouth.

I could feel the flames of my words penetrate her soul; reducing her self-righteousness, into one massive pile of dust beneath her feet. I did not hold back. I pounced – "I'M SELFISH?!" "I am responsible for ruining your Christmas?!" "Let me just tell you how selfish I am. This man you have yourself convinced and everyone else, of being rehabilitated – whom you have somehow chosen to forgive for repeatedly violating me – your daughter – your first born – without ever choosing to consult with me in regards to my position on where I stood with any of it – this person you comfortably have allowed to be under the same roof with your flesh and blood, who has been nothing but emotionally and psychologically triggered since getting off the plane – this man who you were supposedly going to keep an eye on at all times, so as to on some level – offer me assurances of my personal safety – yes, I am so selfish that when he gestured for me to follow him up the stairs to the bedroom – right in-front of Craig and Craig immediately wanting to fly into action – selfish me stopped him – told him to leave the incident alone because I knew that if anything got mentioned, even though I have done nothing wrong – I knew I would somehow wind up getting the brunt of this – the person who would be blamed for what you are now already accusing me of – ruining everyone's Christmas. I was more concerned with allowing you to hold onto your hopes and beliefs that this man was genuinely rehabilitated and not wanting to bring the actual truth to you – so that you – not me – could still somehow enjoy this farce of a holiday. Yeah, that's me being selfish – me putting your make believe fantasy of how normal this family is and how special this holiday reunion is before considering my own physical and emotional well-being. Yeah – a daughter protecting her mother, over a mother protecting her daughter; is selfish. No, there is nothing at all messed up about a mother having her daughter sit beside her abuser at the table for dinner on Christmas Day – completely normal considering the last incident of me being abused, as you already know, also having happened at a table. Are you for real? You're going to put all this on me – again?"

I could not stop – everything unsaid, bottled up and repressed throughout the years – many of her absentee years throughout my life, poured out of me and ricocheted off of her. I had absolutely nothing to lose at this point. I knew the carnage was already too colossal to turn back. I then exploded while in an out of body experience and launched into the series of events that had set in motion, the tangible severing of our physical relationship. I took her and I down memory lane, right back to her having kicked me out of the only childhood home I knew. I was in Grade 10 at the time. My parents had legally separated when I was in Grade 8. My Mum had advocated to hold onto the home 'for the sake of the children,' – to alleviate additional instability and upheaval, during what was already a tumultuous time. She had impressed upon her lawyer, and all involved parties – the importance of her wanting to spare her children (my brother and I) of having to be uprooted from our family home; our close-knit community of Dundas, Ontario, Canada, and thus potentially; our friends and school – the only infrastructure of familiar and in-tact support we had. Her position was also premised on my brother and I being of such impressionable ages and adolescence, already being a challenging period in one's life, never mind anything life-altering being thrown into the mix.

Well, she got her 'maternal/parental' wish and although it was an emotionally difficult time, with adjusting and transitioning to my parents no longer being together and living under the same roof – it was not long after the legalities of our family dynamics becoming officially solidified, that the growing pressures of becoming a single-parent, eventually wore my Mum down. My brother was angry and withdrawn – I was acting out in every which way as a result of unresolved, glossed over sexual abuse, no prevention or intervention, non- existent communication, no suggested counseling or therapy and I knew the ship of Lisa receiving what Lisa so desperately needed, via the adults in her life, in order to find her way again – had sailed once my parent's marriage had completely dissolved.

My Mum had very clearly dipped into a depression. She lacked the where-with-all, energetically, to deal with my brother's emotions, my emotions, coupled with her own emotions. It seemingly became too much for her. I remember many evenings being up in my bedroom – hearing my Mum listening to the same vinyl albums over and over again, while sitting in the dark on the far left corner of the living room couch, clutching a handful of tissues, and often times in those days – nursing her heart with rye and cokes – sobbing inconsolably. Many a time, my name was only called for the purpose of re-starting the needle on the record player for her. The ten steps separating the couch from where the music played, was too much a feat for her. Sad.

I hated how broken we all were – how increasingly disconnected we had all become from one another and from ourselves. If it wasn't a shout fest, it was instead, having to grapple with the constant cloud of darkness that hovered over the entire house; sucking the life and spirit out of each of us. It all came flooding back to me in painful detail, as I stood there in front of her, so many years later, in a different house, in a different country, while going toe-to-toe; tongue-to-tongue; eyeball-to-eyeball with her. I had never known or experienced such intertwined rage and sadness before. I did not even recognize myself or the words that venomously spewed from my mouth. For me, it truly felt like a fight or flight situation, and I was admittedly brutal in that moment. I was out to annihilate her – to hold her accountable – to show her my years of neglected and silenced pain. I wanted to make it abundantly clear in every way that I could, how utterly destroyed and gutted my spirit was, given the unnecessary and avoidable culmination of events and assaults perpetrated against the core fiber of my being.

"You're going to accuse me of being selfish when after you fought to hold onto that house on Sunrise Crescent, you not only kicked both Craig and I out of the house one by one, but you locked up all my stuff in the garage with a padlock, only to later sell off a good portion of my personal and sentimental belongings in your, 'Everything Must Go,' garage sale, when YOU decided to sell the house, get re-married and screw off to the States – leaving no pocket money, no grocery money – no clothing money – no nothing for either Craig or I? Never said good-bye – never attempted to leave on good terms and certainly never considering delaying your departure, until at least seeing or knowing how Craig and I would abruptly have to transition into living in a different city – attending a different high-school half way into the school year, all while winding up on Dad's doorstep, while he was still in the honeymoon phase of his new marriage. What happened to you supposedly giving a shit about mine and Craig's security and stability – the priority of neither of us enduring any more turmoil or upheaval in our lives on top of the divorce itself? All those exact things you screamed bloody murder for with the lawyers? How the hell does a mother abandon her own two children – sell their shit, not say goodbye, sell a family home and hop on a plane to another country to start over with a new man? I'M SELFISH? You know how lost

I have been? How many times I have cried myself to sleep? How many birthday's, Mother's Days and every other holiday, has left me feeling dead inside? How painful back to school shopping was and seeing all the other Mother's and Daughter's celebrating stuff, together? How many times I needed my Mum to talk to about boys, sex, and relationships – to talk about anything and everything? Do you even know that I tried to kill myself by overdosing on anything I could get my hands on and winding up in a hospital drinking charcoal? Do you care at all about what has happened to me in my life? Do you understand on any level how confusing my life has been or how empty I have felt for most of my life?"

There…I had purged, and puked it all out. Gave her the 'Coles Notes' version of this thing called My Life – had rhymed off all the feelings – threw in some f-shots – gave her the up, close, raw and candid version of this hollow shell of a person named Lisa McDonald – her daughter and first born child had been 'surviving' all these years without her.

My anger quickly dissipated and was replaced by instantaneous sorrow – standing in a puddle of tears – rapidly going from being the giant monster in the room, to this now disintegrating, pitiful little girl. Minutes before this all erupted into WW111, I honestly believe I would have physically struck her, had she made any attempt to touch me. Now, with it all out on the floor and me feeling completely spent and dejected – I know I would have welcomed a hug. Perhaps my outburst would have jarred her into feeling a sense of remorse. Maybe she would beg me for forgiveness. Maybe she would offer a heartfelt apology. Maybe she would ask me to consider a new beginning for the two of us. Maybe this is what had to transpire to finally catapult us in the direction of true healing and maybe she would be genuinely committed to wanting to repair our relationship. Maybe she would want nothing more to tell me and wish to convince me of her genuine love for me. Maybe she would ask me for another chance to finally get 'US' right.

All these simultaneous thoughts and deep-seeded wishes bombarded both my heart and my brain. Once again, I found myself staring back at her with pleading, puffy, swollen eyes. Surely, she had to recognize my desperation; my need for her to embrace me as a loving mother should feel compelled to want to do. Through labored breathing that comes when you've just sobbed your guts out – I stood there in what felt like an endless moment in time – anxiously awaiting what was to come.

"Tom!!!" she yelled out to my stepfather. "Tom," she reiterated when he entered the room. "I want her out of here – I want her out of here NOW! Call the airlines and see when we can get her on the next plane." Had she not heard me? Not heard anything I had said? Had she not just witnessed or felt my pain? I could not believe this. Back up to the ceiling I flew – watching this nightmare unfold from a safe distance. I wanted to really and truly die right there – right in front of her. That's not to say that in my heart of hearts that I believed for a second in that exact moment, that it would have changed a damn thing as far as her sheer coldness and complete dismissiveness of me was concerned.

The anger seeped back up again, and with a vengeance. "You're going to kick me out, AGAIN; on Christmas?" "You're going to keep that pedophile here underneath your roof, even with what I just finished telling you what he did – tried to do – wanted to do and you're going to send ME packing?" "Go upstairs to your room!" she barked back at me. "Tom – make the call!" she commanded. "Do NOT talk to your Grandma and do NOT talk to your brother. Go straight to your room until we tell you when you are leaving." "Go pack! Now – GO NOW!"

I was stunned and mortified. I was utterly devastated in a way I had never perceived possible. I thought I had already experienced and understood heartbreak – not even close. Up the stairs I went. I could see the bedroom lights from underneath the doorways in both my Grandma and brother's bedrooms. No one dared to defy my Mum in this moment. Doors remained tightly shut and to my own room, I went.

There was no social media back then – barely cell phones – no computer access – no one for me to reach out to and quite honestly, even if I had any of those things at my disposal, and even withstanding how utterly gutted I had felt – I never would have been so selfish as to have ruined anyone's Christmas just because mine had completely imploded and not just my Christmas, but most profoundly, my hopes and aspirations for a relationship I had so desperately longed for. My mish-mash of competing thoughts was abruptly interrupted with the latest update and development on my impending status. The earliest, next possible flight for me to be on was not until the next morning – Boxing Day around 10:00am.

Before the door was both literally and figuratively shut on me again, I had been forewarned that there was no saying goodbye to either my brother or my Grandma in the morning and that both had been advised of the same – just a quick, swift and immediate exit as if I were some vile, repulsive species who was not worthy of decency or compassion from anyone.

I do not remember whether I did or did not sleep at all that Christmas evening. I do not remember much between the bedroom-door shutting that night to my being dropped off at the airport. I was not allowed to call anyone before being dropped off at the airport – there were no arrangements made on my behalf for anyone to come and claim me on the receiving end. To add insult to injury, I had no choice but to begrudgingly accept monies from them, as I would also need to pay for a bus to get me from the airport back to Dundas. Great! Now I had to muster up the communication skills – put back on the composed – I've-got-my-shit-together; game face so as to navigate through all the superficial conversations and the seeking of information on Boxing Day – just to get what was left of me – 'HOME,' and in one emotional piece.

I did not have a Walkman, or a book, or a pad of paper to feign distraction from potential chitchat with strangers. I was too wired and overtired, to sleep or to pretend to sleep. I sat in my airline seat awaiting takeoff, and as much as I tried to fight back the tears – I just couldn't. They continued to stream down my face. The person sitting beside me was an older woman, and in a very gentle and nurturing voice – leaned in close to me. She had clearly misconstrued my emotional state and said to me, "Saying goodbye to loved ones over the holidays is always a hard thing to do." She rummaged through her purse; handing me a few tissues before kindly leaving me to return to my own thoughts. This woman's compassion for me, matched with seemingly maternal tenderness toward me, only served to reinforce how bottomless my void and how deep my pain.

LIVING FEARLESSLY DOWNLOAD

Do such a phenomenal job loving yourself that if everyone you know was to walk out on you, either one at a time or all at once, that you would be intrinsically strong enough to not only survive, but also find a way to turn that hurt into further developing your INNER-STRENGTH (muscle). No matter how positive, kind, selfless, loving, generous a person you may deem yourself to be, there will be people in this world as you already likely know, who will not choose to like you, love you, accept you, embrace you, or support you. Do not personalize that particularly if they are not respectful enough to use this as a learning/growing opportunity in which, to dialogue with you about whatever their issue or concern may be as it pertains to you. It took me a very long time to realize that people externally view and judge the world in ways, which are indicative to what is going on inside oneself – how they choose to view and judge themselves. Let's face it – owning your own bullshit is not easy or comfortable a process to choose to undertake. Working on oneself with the goal of attaining an improved self, before falling into old, destructive patterns and thought-processes of easily blaming everyone else for your problems or refusing to see yourself as the common denominator in all of your relationships is hard – hard to do and hard to do consistently, but once one commits themselves to understanding that this is a MINDSET – a muscle and practice, which must be honed every single day – until one is committed to understanding that everything begins with self – nothing authentically changes or remains consistently changed for the better or for the betterment of the collective. This is also why I am a huge fan of self-proclamations – I AM, STATEMENTS coupled with MIRROR WORK. These are daily rituals of mine and are as equally important to me as it is to express daily gratitude. What I feed my mind, what I feed my heart, and what I feed my soul, will determine the results and the outcomes in my life. If I want to be loved, I have to love myself. If I want to love others, I have to love myself. If I want to live in a love-filled world, I have to love myself. The message has to be congruent to be authentic. I choose to love myself first and foremost. I am too busying working on bettering myself, to be consumed or pre-occupied with what other people ultimately think about me. And perhaps what other people think of me is none of my business, anyway. IT IS A CHOICE!

Chapter 5

BACK TO REALITY

Once I had touched down on my own turf, I had placed a telephone call to my Dad from the nearest phone booth. I needed to let him know of what transpired, where I currently was, and why. My Dad picked up the phone, sounding distant and not the least bit surprised with receiving the news from me that I had returned back home from the States earlier than scheduled. "I know," he replied. "So what happened?'" he questioned me in an all-too-familiar tone – suggesting he wanted to hear my 'version.'

After choking on the last word of what had happened, there was pause on the other end of the phone. "That's not what I heard," was the response. I was completely perplexed. "What do you mean?" "Who did you talk to? What was said?" I gulped out. "I was told that your behavior was erratic, that you were doing drugs, and that everyone felt uncomfortable continuing to have you underneath their roof, retorted my Dad".

My heart was once again back in my throat as it had not been that long ago, prior to that point in time – that I had broken down in-front of my Dad, disclosing to him that I was not in a great space within any aspect of my life and I was admittedly doing drugs on a fairly regular basis, with the disclaimer however, that I had every intention of walking away from the self-destructive path I was on. I could not conceive the possibility of my Dad thinking, nor believing, that I would lie about what really happened or have him thinking I would actually still be doing drugs – in the States and at my Mum and Step-father's house, no less. HE HAD TO BELIEVE ME! I could not have withstood having both my parents banish me from their lives, in less than a successive twenty-four hour period, to one another and particularly over the Christmas Holidays. I could not have imagined psychologically surviving the back-to-back loss.

I plead with my Dad to believe me. I swore up and down that I was telling the truth – for him to ask either or both, Craig or Grandma for verification if need be. For many reasons – my Dad, my Mum and my stepfather did not all get along during this juncture of time. My Dad told me to call him back shortly. He was going to place a phone call to the States and tell them that I vehemently denied their accusations and reiterate to them what I had shared regarding Reg, the brutal argument between my Mum and I and so forth, as the actual contributing factors to my now being back in Canada earlier than scheduled.

The phone rung on my end as expected. My Dad proceeded to tell me that when he recounted my version of events and had expressed my adamancy as far as my not using drugs or being under the influence of anything at all, that he had then been met with, "Oh, did I say Lisa was doing drugs? What I meant to say was we strongly suspect that Lisa is doing drugs." My Dad in my defense and feeling equally incensed for having been lied to – made it very clear to them that that was not at all what had been initially communicated to him by them. He called them out on it; held them accountable and also took advantage of addressing with them that he thought it completely deplorable and irresponsible how the entire Reg dynamic had been mishandled. He apparently went on to say that, had Reg and I not been underneath the same roof with one another in the first place, that it might be fair to say that the digression between my

Mum and I may not have even unfolded to the degree that it needlessly had. I really loved and appreciated my Dad for having defended me and for being the only adult in this situation, who was the sole voice of reason.

My Dad had immediately been averse to my going to my Mum's home in the first place for Christmas. He was all-too aware of the painfully un-resolved issues; the tumultuous history my Mum and I had on and off shared for many years and had not foreseen anything positive coming out of this trip for my personal well-being. He was absolutely, one hundred percent correct in his overall predictions and assessment of the overall shit-show. And so…another series of milestones, and obstacles would be had for many more years to come, without the presence or knowledge of my Mum. In essence; it was the same old, same old syndrome.

After a few years having gone by, I had received the news that Reg had passed away. Although, conflicted with the internal debate as to whether or not I should chance re-opening Pandora's Box – call me a glutton for punishment, as I did decide to reconnect with my Mum. I picked up the telephone and dialed the number that had been left untouched for what felt like another vacuum of eternity. My hand shook as I heard my Mum's voice on the receiving end.

"Hi Mum, it's me, Lisa." Silence. "I'm calling because I heard Reg died and I wanted to offer you my condolences. How are you?" I managed to nervously spit out. "Why are you really calling me, Lisa? I know that Reg was your least favorite person and you and I have not spoken for years, so why would you out of the blue and for all reasons, want to call ME and offer your condolences because of HIM?" she retorted.

I truly could not win for losing with this woman. Yet, another example that no matter the distance, no matter the circumstances, no matter the mother-daughter connection, or the fact that this woman had a diagnosis with her own mortality facing her in the mirror – it was the defensiveness, the projected coldness that always seemed to dominate and take center stage.

"Regardless of what Reg has done to me, Mum, I know that he was in your life for a long time and because you were able to find it in your heart to have obviously forgiven him for what he did to me (and to many others, both inside and outside of the family – although I refrained from injecting that into the conversation) it is for those reasons I felt it only right to call you and acknowledge your loss." There was a brief pause before being met with, "I'm not sure what your angle is Lisa, but I don't trust it. I have to go now." CLICK.

LIVING FEARLESSLY DOWNLOAD

Sometimes the gift, the message and the lesson for each of us to learn, practice and implement if we are to truly and authentically say that we 'get it' or that we 'got it,' is to be willing to gift ourselves with the plethora of chances and opportunities first and foremost, to 'get things right' with ourselves, before handing out unconditional free passes to everyone else and then wasting precious time and energies by questioning the whys of not receiving the outcomes or the results we were secretly holding out for. I am a staunch believer in the old adage that people will only treat you how you let them. Yes, give people the benefit of the doubt, allow people the opportunity to pleasantly surprise you, allow people the opportunity to do right by themselves and by you, but if by doing so (the first time) results in anything that proves to insult your soul, then be grateful for the lesson and move on and move on in a way that does not rob you with the spirit of still believing in people, in believing people are inherently good, believing in humanity so much that you continue to be open and receptive to affording other people in your path those very same opportunities to shine. This is another form of paying-it-forward and being-of-service to others. The world is only as bright and positive as you deem yourself to be. It is a choice!

CHAPTER 6

DIGGING DEEPER

I eventually grew weary of my life being exactly as it was – how it had been. Everyone was seemingly finding a way to move on with their lives, even if it did not include me. Inside, deep down, I knew I had more to offer – more to do – more to give. Not quite knowing what lay ahead of me or exactly what my goals or life plan should be – not having a road map or a blueprint to work from, and not having or understanding, genuine mentorship at that particular time in my life – I just knew it was more than enough to work with the self-knowledge, and intuitiveness, that I could not withstand one more moment – one more day – one more week or one more year of darkness and nothingness. It was rapidly starting to seep in, to the degree I knew I was wasting my life and losing precious time. I HAD to turn this shit-show around.

From a very young age, I had always been an avid reader. For as far back as I can remember; I had found myself always gravitating toward the self-help/spiritual sections of any particular bookstore or library. Many authors of "How-To Books" – and similar stories of personal anguish and endured hell – truly resonated with me. Scores of these types of books, coupled with a woman named Oprah Winfrey and TV Talk-shows similar to hers (although hers was always the one which resonated with me most) – spoke to me, reached me and touched me deeply – offering me a place of refuge and an atmosphere, which always delivered with respect to me feeling understood and validated. I began to consume, sponge-up the messages, the lessons, and the gifts, which all these beacons of bright-lights imparted to the rest of the world – however; most profoundly what they shared with ME. It truly became daily sustenance and fuel for my soul. I found myself famished and off-center, if I did not receive a daily dose in whatever denomination I could catch – a half an hour here, an entire hour there – a chapter in the morning – a book a week, in many cases. It became a primal need for me, even more than food, sleep or pretty much anything else most humans would deem essential for overall health and well-being.

My appetite increasingly became ferocious, and I non-sparingly, devoured anything and everything accessible to me and at my disposal. The dots in my life rapidly began to connect. I returned to high-school and although I did not graduate with my intended peers – I had more importantly; graduated nonetheless. It was in my final and returning year that I discovered an advanced-level Writer's Craft course, consulted with a Guidance Counselor and it was then, a whole new Universe opened up for me – an entirely new beginning emerged in my daily sphere of reality. I was introduced to a Cooperative Education Placement in the Social Services Department at the CNIB – the Canadian National Institute for the Blind. I was mentored for months by the agencies Social Worker. I had established my first-ever, roster of clients. I had a daily caseload. More importantly – I had PURPOSE. I had DIRECTION and it all related to being of service to others – paying-it-forward. I had been entrusted with a leadership role - and had the responsibility of - connecting with other people's pain and daily challenges – being the conduit in these individual's lives so as to empower them to empower themselves, staunchly advocate for them so that eventually they could in many cases – effectively advocate for themselves. WOW! This was what Oprah was referring to, the Dave Pelzer's of the world (decades later to appear as a guest on my global-reaching weekly radio broadcast show) and the many others who had become my intangible MENTORS – the HEROES, SHEROES, AGENTS OF CHANGE, and THOUGHT-LEADERS of this world. Okay…here was my BLUEPRINT – my road map – my plight – my mission – my journey. I had truly cracked my own code in my own life.

I had subconsciously fumbled my way upon the beginnings of breaking my own silence. I was learning to recognize that I was not alone in my pain, even if other people's pain derived from alternative type circumstances. I got it! PAIN is PAIN and EVERYONE struggles. Every one of us requires the support of others to know how to navigate and maneuver through one's own journey – to master the skill of TURNING SHIT INTO GOLD (talked about this decades later in my talk at Harvard). I had truly hit the UNIVERSAL JACKPOT and from that pivotal, cathartic, turning point – I knew there was no going back to the mindset of having previously felt bleak, directionless as my former self.

I was completely elated when I became educated on what my options were post high-school and knowing there were post-secondary institutions, which offered degree and diploma programs related to my (then) passion of social services as a result of my life-transforming, complete eye-opening CO-OP educational placement at the CNIB.

I knew without a shadow of a doubt, and with zero reservation, hesitation or trepidation, that I was called to be in the field of Social Services. My grades (other than in English, Drama, Parenting Class, Writer's Craft, and now my Co-op placement) were not great. I could not afford University at this juncture of my life. I was living on my own and it was my INTENTION to establish a payment plan with an orthodontist and to soon begin proceeding with the financing of my own much needed and long-overdue braces.

I had applied to Mohawk College where both my Dad and my former stepmother (who has played an active role in mine and my children's lives and who is Nana to the three of us) worked and have both eventually retired from. I had applied to the Social Worker, Early Childhood Education, and the Child and Youth Care Worker Programs. The Child and Youth Worker Program was a three-year diploma program, whereas the other two at the time were both a two-year program. I was out of my body (this time for great reasons) when I had received individual acceptance letters to all three Programs. My Dad has shared with me that this was quite a rarity given that each Program was individually looking for something a little uniquely different in their applicants than all similarly related diploma programs combined. Although, an additional year by comparison – I elected to enroll into the three year Child & Youth Care Worker Program. I was so eagerly excited and grateful to know I would be afforded the opportunity to experience three; four month Co-op Placements within the three year academic experience – working with a variety of populations, all which fell within the 'ISMS.'

I was going to have the honor and the privilege once again, to SERVE others, to EMPOWER others – to be an actual AGENT OF CHANGE – me – Lisa McDonald – go figure! My first placement was at a Women's Shelter – Women and Children fleeing domestic violence. I was responsible for working closely and directly with the children specifically – devising, creating and implementing therapeutic treatment plans and goals for/with each of the children for the duration of their stay in residence. I did this in close consult with the children's mothers so as not to disempower them and assist with providing new and alternative tools for each family's toolbox. In addition, I was responsible for outlining and creating my own professional goals, both long and short term ones – write them out and have them regularly reviewed by both my placement supervisor and the Professor from the College who was monitoring my progress within my placement setting.

I connected the dots again! I was able to recognize that I was receiving tools, practices and guiding principles in all of the self-improvement books I had read and even with what Oprah had reiterated time and time again, which was to journal, write everything down, establish goals for yourself, work toward getting exceptionally clear and still within yourself. These were all key components to revolutionizing myself and for guaranteeing that my self-established goals come to tangible fruition – accompanied with time-lines and the accountability piece of making my goals known to others, and not just myself. When previously identified goals and objectives had in fact been achieved as a result of my first having gotten clear within myself and knowing what my actual setting of intentions were to be, I learnt very quick-ly that it was not enough to stop there – that in order for me to perpetu-ally and consistently grow and evolve, both personally and professionally, I had to internally acknowledge and intrinsically understand that in order to build daily and ongoing momentum, in order to remain fiercely committed to personal growth and development, I had to continually establish newly re-defined targets for myself in-which to reach. There is no end, no being finished as it pertains to and relates to self-improvement and self-actualiza-tion. Was I up for the daily challenge for the rest of my life? You betcha!

From a new bird's eye view and transformed sense of self, I began mor-phing into a person I was truly beginning to love and respect. I became increasingly less concerned with the unfortunate aspects or relationships of my past, which I knew I could not solely change or at all control. This was the beginning of my core understanding of the importance of what it meant for one to surrender and relinquish anything that did not serve my soul or allow me to operate at my highest vibrational level. It was in this phase of my inner journey that I truly began to understand the vital necessity of self-love and self-forgiveness. The more I chose to shed and let go, the more open and receptive I became for my heart, soul, and mind to become fully immersed with what I now term as the yumminess in my life.

I was euphoric, as I was genuinely making a difference in the lives, and spirits of others who I was blessed to cross paths with, both personally and professionally. I quickly learnt that my intended path to help and serve others, was indisputably, and undeniably, my own salvation, and within this spiritual recognition, I was also fortunate to have connected the dots on what it meant for one to authentically honor themselves, and how, by choosing to do so, is one of the most sacred gifts you can lovingly bestow upon your own soul.

My second placement led me to working with teenage boys in a specialized, behavioral classroom – an outdoor portable setting, connected to the property of a community high-school. The boys integrated into the regular, high-school setting a couple of days a week, with the goal of eventual, full-time, on-going re-integration, once anger-management strategies had been fully adopted by each of the adolescent males. A good portion of these individuals, were also living under the care and supervision of The Children's Aid Society, within agency-operated group homes and foster home settings. In-between my first and second placement, I had been offered an actual paid position within my field of study and before even graduating from College with my diploma in hand. I was very fortunate to have been only one of a few classmates to receive this unique opportunity and head start to my career.

I was working at various group and foster home settings and even began taking foster children into my own home (an apartment at the time) for foster-parent relief, per diem weekends. I was paying cash, on my own, each year for my books and tuition and used the monies I had earned from my first ever (summer) job in the field where I had been hired, following my high-school placement with the CNIB (Canadian National Institute for the Blind) to pay for my first year of college, upon learning of my acceptance into all three applied for diploma programs.

The momentum of going in a forward facing, onwards and upward direction, was not only taking massive shape in my life, but was also becoming second-nature for me now. I had learnt how to incorporate and integrate everything I was manifesting, visualizing, honing, and growing from – into my DNA. I was fiercely committed to mastering the ability to get out of my own way and rid myself of the false beliefs and limiting concepts, which beforehand – were not at all serving me with any level of my then – mere-existence. By comparison and in significant contrast, I was now thriving and flourishing. It felt incredibly liberating, empowering, and progressive. I felt ALIVE and it felt equally amazing to know that my inner-brightness and newly harnessed positivity and optimism was having such a profoundly powerful domino ripple effect on those I was interfacing with – in the most spiritually intimate of ways.

Giving and receiving was no longer synonymous with the mired ways of what that, once upon a time, represented for me in the old story of my life, nor did I equate it or parallel it with seediness, dirtiness, violation or intrinsic pain. There was zero shame 'attached' to this form and exchange of reciprocity. Giving and receiving did not have to come at the cost of my soul, my integrity, or my silence. Not only an epiphany for me, but also a massive Universal gift beautifully packaged to me. Gratitude oozed out of me unlike ever before and has thankfully taken up permanent residency in my heart ever since.

My high-school graduation soon turned into my college graduation, which soon turned into my University graduation. My entry-level positions in the field quickly evolved into senior management positions. I went from being a high-school dropout, to being a college practicum student, to eventually becoming the person who hired, mentored, and trained students. I went from being interviewed for jobs and positions to being the one doing the hiring, to conducting performance reviews, re-writing policy and procedure manuals, to participating in Provincial round-table discussions, to collaboratively working on the development and eventual proposal of new legislation. I worked closely with provincial members of parliament and those working and operating also at the federal level to advocate for certain models of cost-effective and quality client-enhanced models of care/housing for some of our most vulnerable populations of individuals. These initiatives received unprecedented funding, removed individuals with special needs from extensive waiting lists, had additional homes built including respite beds, acquired additional dollars for improved staff training and salary-enhancements, and worked tirelessly with one MPP (Member of Provincial Parliament in particular – Cam Jackson who eventually became the Mayor of the City of Burlington where I worked and lived at the time of all these endeavors) to have Bill 125 passed for Ontarians with Disabilities Act.

I continuously threw myself into service, becoming the Chair-Person for Provincial Committees, Spear-Header of Fundraisers, recipient of a Provincial Award from the Alberta Canadian Paraplegic Association – was blessed and honored to have received many glowing letters of commendation – was sought out by agencies for my leadership and skill-sets. I absolutely LOVED what I did because I chose to do what I LOVED, and I did it from the INSIDE-OUT. I learnt very early on, that in-spite of all the gestures of kindness I had received and continue to receive, testimonials, awards, accolades, disclosures, cards, gifts, invitations, offers, referrals, opportunities and ongoing offers to partner and collaborate... although I have been gifted with others immense kindness and gratitude consistently extended to me – if truth be told and as cliché a statement as it is – I truly believe it was each and every person I was blessed to work alongside – every mentor, teacher, student, staff member, client, colleague – every crisis situation I was in the frontlines dealing with head on – every heart-wrenching disclosure, every rape-kit, every trip to court, every resume, life-skill written and crafted – every second of client-advocacy – every trip to the ER, every suicide attempt, incoming crisis-call, every interaction with EMS, every counseling session, and the list goes on...it was the culmination of all these experiences, incidents, perceivable moments of stress, darkness and duress, which gave me much, much more than I believe I ever gave to others, myself.

Every individual person who shared and trusted me with their courage, their scars, their tears, their rage, their secrets, their fears, their rawness and vulnerability – THEIR STORY – it is those HUMAN WARRIORS who have gifted me in my own journey to help 'UNLEASH MY OWN POWER' from within.

LIVING FEARLESSLY DOWNLOAD

I am extremely grateful for having been introduced to 'The Work' by Byron Katie. Amongst many other brilliant sayings, thoughts and concepts, which she shares in her own books, two of my favorites include: "I want for you what you want for you," as well as "It's not your job to like me, it's mine." I believe both to be self-explanatory and quite simply brilliant. I have incorporated much of that mindset into my daily decision-making, not just from a healing perspective, but also with respect to embracing abundance. I choose to view others and myself from the filter and from the lens of we are all inherently good and that this world is fundamentally more bright than dark. It is incredible what happens to the evolution of one's own self-esteem, self-confidence, and our overall outlook on the world in general, when one operates from a place of focusing energies on what is exactly right with the world – on what is exactly right with ourselves and on what is exactly right with anything and anyone external to ourselves. It is the mirroring effect – I choose to see in you, what I equally choose to see in myself. I will always choose Love over Fear. IT IS A CHOICE!

CHAPTER 7

MET MY MATCH

One of my most profound personal and professional growth opportunities which I bitter-sweetly jumped into (another example of how I semi-consciously relinquished fear and just STEPPED-INTO-IT) presented itself to me through word of mouth when I was in my 20's. I was hungrily embracing academia, workshops, masterminds, courses – anything and everything I could sink my teeth into.

I had been encouraged to look into an Advanced Clinical Internship Program offered by a Social Service Agency in Oakville, Ontario (HCC-SA – Halton Childhood Centre for Childhood Sexual Abuse). This was an agency whose niche and specialty was working with sexual abuse survivors. The Internship was divided into two distinct categories – Basic and Advanced, based upon accreditation, length of years and success within the field, references, having established a proven working clinical knowledge and history on the subject matter.

Me being exactly who I am – I chose to by-pass the prescribed criteria and submitted my lengthy and very detailed application, inclusive of an autobiographical essay, documentation, certificates, degrees, references, etc., followed up with an intensely grueling face-to-face interview with the Clinical Executive Director of the Agency, Edith Sands, whose presence immediately oozed of respect, wisdom and intelligence. It was admittedly one of the most intimidating professional experiences of my career – simply because I knew I was being rigorously interviewed by a powerhouse woman who exuded self-empowerment.

At the end of the Q & A with Edith, she respectfully cited her reasons as to why she believed I was not ready to be one of the eleven candidates accepted into the Advanced Level, eleven month, Advanced Clinical Internship Program. She was extremely forthcoming and genuine in her feedback, saying such things like, she respected my bravery and courage for applying, and that she loved my gumption and self-assuredness. Edith had asked me if I had any final questions for her before concluding our rigorously, intensive, in-person, interview.

"I do actually have a question for you, Edith," I blurted out. "I would like to know what I can do, should do, have to do, to change your mind, and to prove to you that I not only deserve to be one of the eleven successful candidates chosen, but to also show you that I want this opportunity probably more than anyone else who is applying or being considered. I know I am the youngest of the bunch, and the most professionally in-experienced."

"Keep talking," Edith responded.

"I promise you, Edith, I will work twice as hard as anyone else – I will not miss one session for the entire eleven month duration of this Internship. I will learn everything there is to possibly learn. I will be present with the team and the clients. I am so committed to this, Edith. I need to do this for my own growth and development as a professional so as to properly and effectively serve others and do it with justice," I convincingly and genuinely plead.

Edith looked at me and said, "If accepted as one of the eleven interns, you would have the choice, as would the other ten interns, to co-counsel clients with your appointed Mentor with the following population, choices:

» Female Children Survivors

» Female Teenage Survivors

» Female Adult Survivors

» Male Children Survivors

» Male Teenage Survivors

» Male Adult Survivors

OR…the last group

*Male Sexual Offenders who are mandated by the Courts to receive group therapy. Which group would you choose to work with and why?" I instantly responded with my answer. "I would only want to work with the male sexual offenders; my reason for that being, two-fold. I have already been fortunate so far in my short-term career within the field, to have worked with both children and adolescents who have been sexually abused – both male and female. I have worked with women who have been on the spectrum of abuse, including sexual abuse. Knowing where I want to go and where I see myself within my future career – the only way I can be credible, and professional, is for me to work closely with the men so that I can gain a deeper insight into the psyche of a predator/pedophile. I have to especially work closely with them in light of my own sexual abuse history. For me – if I cannot effectively work the whole entire spectrum of abuse and who falls on either side of it, then within myself, I will not consider myself to be a true professional even if others do." That was it. That was my answer. That was my core truth.

Edith and I sat in reflective silence for what felt like an eternity to me. I believed I was also being tested on how comfortable I could be sitting in lengthy silence – a necessity I knew, respected and understood for this level of co-counseling. The silence was growing increasingly uncomfortable for me, but I did not dare interrupt it. Here it comes! I braced myself as Edith opened her mouth to begin speaking.

"Lisa, I like you…a lot. You have more courage and magic about you than I believe you are aware of. I want you to know and be prepared for the reality that you are going to be triggered. I want you to be prepared for the fact you will be the only female in the room. The group as you know will consist of all men and your mentor, whom you will be co-leading and co-counseling the group with, is also male. You are going to be exposed to hearing all kinds of graphic disclosures and intimate details. These men are masters at manipulation. They are for the most part, not here on their own volition. These men will likely attempt to sexualize you, intimidate you, and demean you in the way of dynamics, posturing, and non-verbal body language. It will be up to you to confidently and convincingly, assert your own boundaries and leadership, to rise above it and to claim your own power, role and position within the group, if you are going to gain the full and optimal experience from this learning opportunity. We (the Team) are all here to do mandatory de-briefing and check-ins with one another, prior to and following each weekly session throughout the eleven-month internship. It will be each intern's responsibility to stick it out for the entire eleven months – no requests to transfer to another group of choice. Once you are committed to your choice of group, you will see it through with that same group from beginning to end. You truly believe you are mentally prepared for this?"

"Yes, Edith. I AM. I understand everything you have just stated." With that, Edith shook my hand, gave me a hug and said, "Welcome." I remember thinking to myself; I wish Oprah could have just witnessed this moment in my life. I believed she would have been proud of what she calls and refers to as the 'A-ha' Moment. One day!

Well, be careful what you wish for right?! Everything Edith had itemized of what I could anticipate to unfold within the group – did.

I have always appeared to look more youthful than my actual chronological years. It did not help that I was also adorning a mouthful of braces, given I could not afford them on my own, until later in life. So here I was, the only female in the room, looking like a teenaged metal-mouth, who likely and quite insultingly to these men, was in a position of authority and leadership. Quite possibly it might have been more amusing to them than anything else. I knew I was the underdog of the group, the brunt of the joke, if you will.

As perplexing a concept to the average mindset outside of this particular realm of profession, it was my job and my job alone to earn the respect and trust of these men, regardless of what they had individually and collectively perpetrated on many they came into contact with, in both their personal and professional lives of whose lives they had turned upside down and inside out – no matter the scars, the heinous crimes of what they had committed against their students, own clients, children, grandchildren, nieces, nephews, siblings and also those at random, to whom they had no personal connection or history with. It was ME who had to earn THEIR trust and respect. I was the outsider who had to pave my way to them.

About two months in, one of the youngest members of the group, even though much older than myself, looked right at me as it was his turn to SHARE in the group. As he stared right at me, almost through me, he said to me, "You know, Lisa, you remind me an awful lot of my beautiful wife." That comment in and of itself might have been enough to make anyone in my position want to bolt. However, that was nothing in comparison to in actuality, how loaded of a statement it truly was, as what this man had previously disclosed openly to the group in one of our sessions, was that he was in the group because of what he had self-admittedly done to his wife that led him to being here with us. He had been charged with repeatedly sexually assaulting his wife, while she was asleep (yes, this does and can happen. A person can in fact be violated while in an un-awakened state – initially or throughout the entire duration of the assault).

This man who had confessed to raping his wife in her sleep and disclosing with minimal expression of grief or remorse, so it seemed, was now locked in on me and saying I reminded him of his beautiful wife. On a platter, this fight or flight, kill or be killed, do or die moment was being presented to me. Back up to the four corners, I flew. ALL eyes were on me, including those of my mentor who was consciously choosing not to step-in as he knew to have done so, would have been completely dis-empowering and would have flushed my internship experience down the toilet. This was my golden ticket into complete and total acceptance into the group. I did a quick self-inventory – un-peeled myself from the four corners of the ceiling – fully aligned myself in the moment, leaned further forward on my chair, made sure my arms were not crossed, that my shoulders were fully back and my posture was upright and I eye-balled, 'Joe' straight on; matching his intensity.

"Well, Joe – I take what you have just said to me as a compliment. Your wife sounds like an incredibly strong and courageous woman and not only for what she has endured as a result of what you have put her through, but also because she proceeded with the tough and unfair decision to hold you – her husband and father to her children – accountable by pressing charges against you. That is exactly the type of woman I would consider an honor to be compared to on any given day, so thank you for that."

I was convinced everyone in the room could hear my heart pounding. I felt my body in full-on perspiration mode. I knew I had held my composure well. I knew my tone was calm and I knew my message was professionally delivered. What I did not know in that precise moment was how it would be received. Joe gave me a once-over, two of the other men in the group had laughed out-loud, while looking directly at Joe – awaiting and gauging his anticipated reaction/response. My mentor winked at me with a look on his face, which I read to mean, 'slam-dunk.' Everyone in the room knew this was a defining moment. All eyes were now off of me and instead; fixated on Joe. Joe looking a little caught off-guard and momentarily lost for words; came back at me with, "You're alright, Lisa."

Those words spoken aloud to me in the group, was validation and confirmation that I had passed my 'initiation test.' This exchange between Joe and I, had cemented my acceptance into the group and this rung true for the remaining ten months of that clinical internship. I had confronted my fears, yet again, and had elevated myself to another level of (ongoing) healing, personal empowerment, personal growth and self-development. I had now proven to myself, which was my ultimate objective, that through fighting my way for a spot, that I could one hundred percent, professionally and effectively work with any and all prospective client-populations.

LIVING FEARLESSLY DOWNLOAD

Choosing to jump back into the fire, as some may say, I metaphorically did, when electing to co-counsel the male sexual offenders, as opposed to any other client group offered or available to me, is exactly what I believe I needed to do, but also what one needs to do in the overall, bigger stage of life in order to grow. I hadn't even framed it to myself in such a way as though I were facing my fears so to speak, rather, I had framed it in such a way to myself and to others (the power of language) that if I was going to both internally and externally (congruency) deem myself (more importantly) and be deemed by others as professionally sound to effectively and to appropriately work with ALL client populations, then I had to challenge myself that I in fact could by eliciting this opportunity for myself (mindset). How we frame things and dialogue with ourselves, will very much determine one's own personal growth. IT IS A CHOICE!

CHAPTER 8

MY OWN BATTLE WITH CANCER

I had not long prior to graduating from college, received the telephone call in September of 1994 - my Mum had been diagnosed with Stage III aggressive breast cancer. Compassionate Lisa always did and always will feel, and even since the 2014 passing of my Mum – a genuine sadness for what she grappled with physically as a result of her twenty-plus year journey with the disease. No one should have to contend with invasive procedures and surgeries, cocktails of various chemo's and radiation treatments, and toward the latter years, even being re-introduced to chemo's, which had already expired their once before effectiveness and longevity, but when not selected for Clinical Trials, trying anything a second or third time for maintenance purposes and additional time, was the path my Mum had chosen for herself.

The diagnosis is what had physically re-united my Mum and me once again and after many years of prior estrangement. I will always give my Mum credit for her indomitable spirit and amazingly positive attitude she embodied in the face of her journey with cancer. She had become a role model and mentor for those newly diagnosed, who had also participated in the support group sessions my Mum had regularly attended. My Mum had been one of the Public American Breast Cancer Ambassadors.

She had been interviewed on television, been a speaker at cancer related events, had knitted and crocheted lap blankets for both Veterans and for those undergoing chemo treatments. She was known for her declaration of cancer not being an automatic death sentence. She had been living proof of that – had been told by various oncologists and surgeons that she was an anomaly. Statistically speaking, for all she went through and endured and for how aggressive her cancer was said to have been, living as long as she did post initial diagnosis, year-to-year for a total of an additional 20 plus years – was said to have been extremely rare. Doctors and those on the medical team involved in my Mum's care, had commended her on her stellar attitude as one of the key, precipitating factors for defying such statistical odds for each additional day and year she had remained here amongst us.

At the risk of sounding cold and perhaps cruel – I had only reached out to my Mum upon my receiving the news of her initial diagnosis, as I truly wished for her to depart this realm of existence having known it was important to me to wish her well in the next phase of her journey, knowing that transitioning over could be upon her at any-time (as is true for all of us but perhaps more accelerated a pace when one is working with an actual diagnosis). I genuinely wished for her to feel absolved of any perceivably unspoken guilt she may have been carrying around inside herself. I wished for her to have felt and received some form of closure or sense of being forgiven, for her role and participation in our relationship for things we could not mutually change or turn the clock back on. I had reinserted myself back into the fold only for these reasons – for her well-being and peace of mind, as well as for my own. I truly believed she was not far from being on her way out back then and it felt like the humane, well-intentioned, and necessary step to take. I had not reached out to my Mum wishing to resurrect another attempt at establishing a so-called relationship or to embark upon a new beginning so to speak. It had de-spirited me to the core, and I had travelled so far in my own healing journey. I had made leaps and bounds in my initial reinvention process – really at that juncture just trying to find my own way in this world and to healthily carve out a spot for myself. I only wished to seek out the right people to align myself with – aspiring to feel and be positive and genuinely proud of myself as I continued to develop the pattern and habit of doing all these right things for myself. I was re-programming myself with new and healthy daily rituals and I was fiercely committed to honing and remaining emotionally connected to myself day in and day out in going forward. Going backwards on any level was not an option and not something I ever contemplated or pondered. I was done with it all.

My primal instincts had become more refined. I had understood the importance of asserting personal boundaries mainly for self-preservation purposes. I also equally understood the necessity to keep and maintain a safe distance from anything and anyone who posed a legitimate threat to my well-being. It honestly had not felt healthy or even intuitively possible for me to again incorporate my Mum back into my life or to merge her with my newfound sense of reality. I had worked extremely hard at the deepest of intrinsic levels to have carved out and created my new lease on life.

Not many people who had mutually known both my Mum and I, had known the intimate details of our relationships history, struggles or the underlying taboo details, which were at the center of my childhood – did they seem to know, we were always on and off for indefinite periods of time. What everyone knew now at this particular juncture was that my Mum had been diagnosed with Stage III aggressive breast cancer. I now had a uniquely, new battle on my hands; also clutching at my conscience. Never mind what kind of daughter I would have been questioned to have been in the eyes of everyone – if I had chosen not to put our so-called 'differences' aside and instead, focus on the so-called 'bigger picture' of what should perceivably matter (at least from an optics standpoint, alone) had I opted not to step-up and step-in where my Mum and her cancer was concerned, but the bigger question might have been, but what kind of human being would Lisa McDonald be – this person who is seemingly committed to working in the trenches for every other sector of 'client' population – with all of their inner struggles and personal afflictions and hardships – just how authentic is Lisa McDonald, really, if she pours all of her energies and compassion into initial strangers, but not for her own flesh and blood?

I was contending with this controversy and inner battle on a bigger stage now, given my Mum lived in the States and because she was revered and admired as this larger-than-life cancer-warrior and was an Ambassador of the Breast Cancer Association/Community, and because of our lengthy, on-going periods of strife and estrangement – many of these people who treated her like a Martyr/Guru – these same people who did not have long-standing history with her or to have known her prior to her choosing to abandon her children in Canada – opting for an easier, a more stress-free, less-encumbered life in the USA – they did not know me or my story or hers and our story, nor did they know of the 'CANCERS' in my life. The 'CANCERS' I had desperately been trying to rid my own body and spirit of. My prescribed treatment regimen for trying to shrink my own (spiritual) tumors was to detoxify myself from the cumulative negativity – the 'triggers,' which had accelerated my own cells into chaotic and psychological hell and had been known to advance my own risk factors related to aggressive diagnosis and long-term prognosis. What about my right to question or value my own quality vs. quantity of life and decision-making processes? Why couldn't I be allowed to respectfully be entitled to the exact same rights to healthily choose for myself without it coming under scrutiny or to the detriment of myself likely imploding again and eroding my own 'treatment' measures and gains and successes to date if being the dutiful, compassionate daughter had or should be the ultimate priority in this situation – should be what takes ultimate precedence?

For those who know me well enough to know the emotional tight-rope I walked with all of this – and not necessarily with the knowledge of knowing all the dark and sordid details, which exacerbated my inner-struggle and who still respectfully extended their deep-felt sympathies and compassions for how difficult it must have been to be me, I say: thank you. Having a mother who was diagnosed with aggressive cancer – I can honestly say that any sadness I felt at that particular period in my life, was actually foreshadowed by resentment. I was more resentful of my Mum than ever-before. I was resentful that I was even in that energetic space, when I was doing so well in just simply minding my own business and truly only focused on growing and advancing my own self, while rising out of the ashes of the past. I believe I had a deeper hate-on for cancer, than most people typically do or would as I felt my Mum having cancer was going to equate to my own death sentence. I felt once again, emotionally held hostage and hijacked from Lisa, simply being allowed to be Lisa and live Lisa's own life – a life filled with new beginnings and more light-hearted possibilities.

Truthfully, how does someone walk back into someone's life, only to say goodbye and then walk back out when they are still alive?

I was not as evolved back then, as I would like to believe myself to be now, to know I was not obligated to rip apart my own soul to shreds in order to put my Mum and her journey ahead of my own. I was not truly operating from a place of self-love or a graduated sense of self-awareness, when I begrudgingly chose to ignore my own inner voice, intuition and gut instincts. However, in the saying of that, I regret nothing in my life as chances are, this book would not be writing itself had I changed course at any juncture of my life's journey and the plethora of life-lessons I have learnt along the way – albeit – many of them excruciatingly painful. I would not have transcended into the person I now proudly, AM.

Therefore, in traditional Lisa fashion, I dove back into the time-warp, déjà vu, groundhog-day that had become the all-too familiar patterns of my life, while delicately trying to 'balance' the one foot I had in one world and the other foot I was fighting to keep grounded in the other. Existing within simultaneous and dual realities was nothing new for me and so back in the ring, I went.

I watched my Mum deliver her speech at the podium of a breast cancer event she had been asked to keynote in Buffalo, NY, where she lived at the time. It was a large sold out venue. I sat at a round table with many of my Mum's biggest advocates and cheerleaders. I watched each of them as they all took in her every word, whilst in complete awe of her. There were many gasps, ooh's and ah's in the audience before the entire room erupted into a lengthy round of applause, while all on their feet. The deep-seeded resentment was once again rearing its ugly head. How lovely all these people got to publicly acknowledge their individual battle with the ugly C-word – how liberating and empowering for each of them that all their trials and tribulations and hellish disclosures were met with embracing warmth and affections – the reciprocal exchanges of familiar and all-knowing facial expressions and non-verbal body language. How amazingly bonding and special that these hundreds of people could safely and comfortably congregate and rally together as a unified voice – a unified front in sisterhood type solidarity and converse ad nauseam about their darkest moments that had altered every aspect of their lives and had screwed with their psyche, and had invaded their spirits. How magnificently special that this commonly spoken about topic – CANCER – could be spewed in never-ending dialogue and no one had to secretly cringe at the repeated mentioning of the word itself.

They had all found a place to flock, to support one another and wave the recognizable pink ribbon banner of connectedness. I was happy to see my Mum swimming in this pool of camaraderie, validation and unification. How lovely it must have been and felt for her to be on the receiving end of un-ending support, un-wavering compassion, and unconditional love. I made introductions with all members of my Mum's raw-raw, cheerleading camp. Here I was – this grown woman, the daughter of their beloved, Jenny, who had never before been seen, who these people did not truly or genuinely know, watching and witnessing my Mum being fawned over. I found it peculiar and quite odd that all these people who doted on my Mum and who seemingly idolized her, that for all the perceivable reasons of why my Mum resonated with them, and based upon her being regarded as the epitome of positivity, how they could not be the least bit curious or objective as to why she had this on and off estranged, bittersweet relationship with this daughter of hers – someone who was also equally giving back and being of service and not solely to my tribe of incest survivors but to the collective. Anyone else here, other than me, able to play devil's advocate or dig deeper beyond the surface, I silently wondered to myself.

As if being in this arena was not emotionally challenging enough for me, I was then immersed in forthcoming post-speech congratulatory wishes extended to my Mum. "You are such an inspiration, Jenny! We love you, Jenny! I am so proud to know you, Jenny! We cannot thank you enough for all you do for us, Jenny! There is no one quite like you, Jenny!" Ingesting all of this was wreaking havoc on all of my senses and literally made me feel physically ill.

"This is my daughter, Lisa, from Canada," while on cue, I robotically extended my hand to the sea of pink people. My face was starting to hurt from the over-forced smile I kept plastered upon my face. The un-naturalness of this was making my head pound. "You must be so extremely proud of your Mum, Lisa. Isn't she such a pillar of strength and positivity for all of us?" "This must be so difficult for you, Lisa, as it is for all of our family members. When one member of the family gets cancer – it affects each and every one within the family as a whole." This line of rhetoric was endless. All I could think of was how much longer I could withstand this. I was literally feeling physically impacted. I felt wobbly on my feet as if I might spontaneously black out at any given moment. I was acutely aware of all my bodily rhythms speeding up, as well as my bodily senses morphing into overload.

Once again, an example of others being completely oblivious and immune to my inner chaos. Was I the only one who could non-verbally read others? Sense other people being off-kilter within my immediate surroundings? Was I the only one tapped into in-congruencies in other people's mannerisms and interactions? Here I was, standing beside my Mum, swarmed by a room full of women who all seemed a-tune to each other's pain and myriad of emotions all shared and felt by each of them. There was no shortage of disclosure or testimonial to support this. I was the fork in the middle of this cancer highway – getting hit with it from all four directions. Even without a diagnosis, I was fighting for my own survival just as fiercely as these pink warriors.

I cannot recall the name of the lovely woman who was gracious enough to kindly switch gears, when she asked questions about me. "What do you do for a living up in Canada, Lisa?" It was beautifully timed, given all that I was internally battling, while trying to hold my own at this event.

"I am a Child and Youth Care Counselor. I work in group and foster home settings with children and teenagers who have been abused physically, mentally, emotionally, psychologically, spiritually, and sexually." I purposely attached the 'sexually' at the tail end of my response so it would linger and hopefully resonate, if not with these other women, but at the very least, with my Mum. This is not to suggest that the other women would in any way, shape or form, be insensitive or oblivious to the plights and challenges of others on the outside of cancer, but unbeknownst to them, it was a subtle reminder to my Mum that I still had my own battle wounds and scars and with a subject matter that was still taboo for her to ever comfortably resurrect.

Cancer could be talked about for hours, days, weeks, months, and years on end as was the ongoing case in my family, but what happened to me (and what I would later come to learn – with it being ALLOWED to happen to me) was blatantly an over and done with chapter in everyone else's lives, especially if it was not still actively happening to me therefore there was no justifiable reason to still dwell on it. Very interesting that there was no ceiling or expiration date associated with un-ending discussions related to side effects, treatments, support groups, walks, fundraising, fellow survivors, stats, quality of life and so forth as it pertained to my Mum's sole journey with cancer, but not once was I ever offered the option, the suggestion or even the parental reinforcements of what might have been in my best interest for my overall health. I was not encouraged on any level or at any phase of my life to elicit any form of external support system for myself, even as a secondary option to what one might primarily expect to receive from their family infrastructure of support system, first and foremost. Conversely, I was completely left in the dark by anyone and everyone who one might be inclined to believe; should have instinctively stepped up and stepped in with an innocent child desperately requiring a life-line.

I would have loved and very much appreciated, if someone – anyone – who claimed to have given a shit about Lisa McDonald and her well-being, could have – would have – made a referral for me – had taken the initiative or the lead role in pairing me with a therapist, a counselor, a support group – if for at the very least and for no other reason than to have lovingly reinforced to me, that I was not the only person in this world whom these awful and sickening things had happened to. The sexual abuse itself was only one component of this cumulative domino effect involving the chain of events, which I ultimately had to completely face on my own (at least from an emotional standpoint).

Where was the EMOTIONAL INTELLIGENCE on this one? Where was the parental RESPONSIBILITY and ACCOUNTABILITY in any of this? How could anything un-raveling in either of my family's/parents lives – no matter how dark, no matter how personally painful or seemingly insurmountable within their own level of struggle and hardship, supersede the priority of ensuring your own child's physical safety? And in the knowledge of eventually learning to whatever degree one parent may have been completely oblivious, how then and not at the very least, does immediate swift action to secure follow up supports for your child, also get conveniently, quietly, and secretly dismissed and swept under the rug as well? Where is the FORESIGHT as an adult, as a caregiver or as a parent to not anticipate, predict or connect the dots on CAUSE and EFFECT? How does one convince themselves that an injured child should receive zero access to a triage of intervention? How does an adult in this situation not have their parental instincts or mind race to all the hellish concerns, worries, paranoia, worst case scenarios of churning over what the future ramifications may be for their child if left untreated, if left un-discussed, if left to their own child's devices and with minimal resources? What parent does not view it as their inherent responsibility to go to the ends of the earth to exercise some level of due diligence and at the very least, have their child go forward in life with the best First Aid Kit possible so as to alleviate or lessen additional and unnecessary trauma – call it self-esteem, future relationships, self-concept, self-worth, trust and confidence building/re-building, how to effectively deal with triggers rather than running the risk of your child self-sabotaging, imploding, becoming self-destructive, suicidal or grappling with suicidal ideation, elevated risk of addictions, the menu goes on. How does a parents mind not go there intuitively and instinctively? How does an immediate call to action not happen? How does damage control not make the radar? How can a child turned teenager, turned adult, turned adult without children, turned adult with children GRASP THIS, yet the adults in this situation could not?

It became abundantly evident that I was truly on my own with what I had to do, to stockpile my own arsenal with strategies, tools, love, compassion, empathy, solutions, and intervention, if I was ever going to make it in this world and come out better and stronger on the other end of it. It was clearly up to me to figure out how to get on the right side of the tracks if I was ever to stand a realistic chance of turning my life around. I had to once and for all, stop banging my head against the wall and discontinue my own toxic contribution to this dysfunction with the would of, could of, should of with all the characters within the story – it was moot. It was irrelevant. I had now entered into the terrain of what was Lisa prepared to do for Lisa to change the story, to re-write the story, to produce different outcomes, to become her own SHERO, her own LEADER in her own LIFE. This was my responsibility and my choice. This was my gateway to eternal freedom. This was my gift to myself. I distanced myself from the old diatribe of no one cares about me, no one loves me, no one values me, and no one protects me or looks out for me. I was on a MISSION to disseminate, dismantle, and eradicate all the toxins and perceivable cancers in my own life. I was committed to holding myself accountable for obtaining and achieving my own healing, my own happiness, my own truth, my own fulfillment, my own vision, and to accomplish this by also seeking to find my own TRIBE.

The old story and details of being sexually abused, being a child of divorce, being kicked out of houses and schools, having what little I had in the way of sentimental items (reminders and tokens of happier times in my life) being sold at garage sales, being walked out on, having little infrastructure of familial support and guidance and everything else that unfolded for me…was DONE. I chose to focus on how these circumstances helped to shape and mold me into a more empathetic, compassionate, kinder, human being. To shift my mindset to a place of recognizing that everything that happened in my life was in fact gifts bestowed upon me to be of more authentic service to others who were perhaps still stuck in the mindset of victim– of feeling sorry for themselves of seeing no way out, who perhaps felt stuck and on the fence in their own lives. Others who were perhaps keeping themselves small, playing small, remaining invisible, remaining unheard and remaining unseen in their own lives. Others who wanted, but did not necessarily know how to reinvent themselves, their lives, re-write their own story, shift their own mindset, alter their own self-dialoguing patterns, or who had forgotten how to love themselves or even know where to start toward choosing something different – something better. I became fiercely committed to de-programming, de-constructing; de-mystifying all the former indoctrination, false and limiting beliefs, which no- longer served me, nor would continue to hold power over me. By choosing to manifest this for myself, not only would I become the best possible version of myself, but I would also have the capabilities of reaching the masses with respect to being another human example of how it can be done, that it can be done, and how each of us can master these essential ingredients and incorporate them into our own DNA so as to raise the collective consciousness and for us all to become meaningful contributors in this world as opposed to destructive contaminators. I know now as I knew then, what I am here to do on this planet.

TIME TO GET BUSY!

LIVING FEARLESSLY DOWNLOAD

It is a gift when we can choose to shift our focus to discovering and un-leashing the hidden gem of a message, the golden nugget, the lesson. Process of elimination and the ability to discern, that which most resonates with our soul as compared to what, does not, is also a great barometer for figuring ourselves out. In the example of my Mum, I had to really work on not becoming fixated or consumed or angry for the ways in which I perceived or internalized her indifferences to me. Rather than, chance losing myself in the unknowns of things that did not make sense to me or try to change or fix what was never within my control to begin with, I worked extremely hard at being grateful for the gift of contrasting and discerning qualities as well as characteristics – those which resonated with me and choosing to adopt what worked – and alternatively – rejecting those same qualities and characteristics, which did not resonate with me. I worked diligently on this area of growth, specifically as it was the one I was always most challenged by. My approach became how one simply approaches an open buffet table. As objectively as I possibly could, I would look at the smorgasbord and assortment of qualities and characteristics and as I made my rounds looking, assessing and evaluating what I wished to add to my plate – what I deemed to be yummy, and beneficial, and nourishing for my soul. I would then focus my energies there, while not turning a blind eye to also acknowledging the importance of what would not be good for my health – what I already knew I had an aversion to, what would likely cause me to have an upset stomach, what I was perhaps somewhat 'allergic' to and not wanting to chance an unnecessary negative reaction by putting things into my body (body, mind, spirit – all one) that would cause me to feel ill as opposed to nourished and properly fed. It was my choice and my responsibility what I decided to put on my own plate. IT IS A CHOICE!

CHAPTER 9

THE PURSUIT OF PURPOSE

From a very young age, I was fully aware of my genuine fascination and curiosity for how one portion of humanity could endure the most catastrophic, painful, heinous, and inconceivable of in-justices and re-markably, and often times unexplainably, be the exact same individuals who rose from the ashes and did whatever was required to turn it all into something extraordinarily brilliant and not just for themselves, but for others. It is a super-human strength, a quality, a spirit, and a magic that defies logic or even adequate description. In drawing from my own examples, I often times fondly remember many of the women who came through the doors of the Women's Shelters I had managed once upon a time. In many cases, these were women who entered the shelter with only the clothes on their back and the backs of their accompanying children. English was not their first language, sometimes not even their second. Some of these women had not graduated with their GED – had no access to monies, were not in possession of legal documents, such as a Health Card, Birth Certificates, Social Insurance Numbers, in many cases were not allowed to work or be independent in any respects, did not have a driver's license or a vehicle – had been living in the most dire, destitute and desperate of circumstances and yet...these women/mothers kicked it into high gear to protect themselves and their children from enduring further abuses and atrocities by choosing to seek refuge elsewhere. From a devil's advocate perspective, these women would be able to very easily justify remaining in their current situations, as they would be able to rationalize it as familiar, perhaps basic needs, survival such as having a roof over their heads, one source of consistent income coming in alleviating some of the stressors they would not have to worry about additionally inheriting if fleeing their homes. Instead, instinct kicked in. Self-preservation kicked in no matter the up-hill battle.

I contrast these women's unimaginable hardships and the unfair position of having to make brutal, split-second decisions, all hinging on life and death in some cases to that of what went down in my own childhood and in my own home. These women, who had nothing in the way of monies, resources, education, or support, still knew what the right thing was to do in regards to their children being put first. They took massive action and demonstrated genuine leadership and did so, while being in personal crises, while being emotional wrecks themselves and not knowing up from down and with not being able to think outside of the immediate moment itself. They assumed personal responsibility, accountability and inherent ownership for their roles as mothers/parents and essentially – role models to their children. They took decisive action for their children and their futures. If these women could grasp the basic concepts that underscored their own children's rights and need for protection, when they did not have a pot to piss in, what then was my family's excuse or any family that mimicked mine? It truly was mind-blowing to me.

Back to the lovely woman in my Mum's pom-pom squad, who cared enough to kindly enquire about me. My answer of what I did for a living hung open in the silence for a moment and not without my noticing the immediate change to my Mum's demeanor. Probably completely un-recognizable and undetected by the other women, but all too familiar a disposition to me. Body language really does scream out the un-spoken truths! My vocational choice and any discussion or updates pertaining to the underbellies of real life shit that mirrored my own life or that of mine and my Mum's relationship was unsurprisingly, not a subject matter that was either initiated or embraced by my Mum. Everything I did for a living – projects, committees, fundraisers, advocacy-work, client-care, staff training and so forth, was a slippery slope and a fine-line for the two of us. Everything I stood for, believed in, worked toward and had already achieved in my life, was clearly rooted in the parallels of our own dysfunction – she knew it and I knew it. The more I spoke about my life, my passions, my endeavors, and my goals, the more she cowered away and kept it all at arm's-length. Ironically, it would also mark the stronger ramping up of the Cancer Card.

I honestly believed that my Mum receiving a cancer diagnosis would be the cure-all for our relationship-ills. And every-time there was a recurrence, or a failed chemo-intervention or even metastases, I was further convinced it would lead my Mum one step closer toward self-awareness, lead the two of us one step closer toward healing wounds and ridding ourselves of our own cancerous relationship. I envisioned a huge emotional breakthrough – the most cathartic of transformations, the most profound of mindset shifts, a new beginning – a renewed mother/daughter connection between the two of us. Unfortunately, as much as I held out for this and did whatever I thought I could to make this a feasible possibility or reality for us, it wasn't in the cards. It never came to be.

When my Mum received un-favorable or disappointing news from the oncologist(s), any light-bulb or 'a-ha' moments I thought I had gleaned or thought to have bore witness to, seemingly evaporated and was instead, replaced with her own plight/mission to make the most of her own life, exclusive of me or the betterment of our relationship. The attention, energies and focus was not on us, rather, it returned to the wonderfully kind gestures of knitting and crocheting lap blankets for ultimate strangers, all of which was genuinely lovely and altruistic in-spite of my own inability to comprehend why remedying our relationship in the face of death was not a mutual priority, nor seemingly – a maternal need or instinct to want to strive for. I tried on many an occasion to objectively understand why, from her own perspective, never mind mine – why this was not innately important to her. It was her diagnosis, her own mortality looking back at her in the face on a daily basis, she was the parent, she was the adult, and I was her 'baby.' Why was this more my concern or thought process as the child than for her as the parent/mother?

Being a mother myself, the mere thought of either of my two beautiful children ever on any level or for any reason, questioning my love or commitment to them or believing I had injured their souls, hearts or spirits or that I did not value or respect them as human beings, would just about do me in – especially, if I knew in my heart-of-hearts, that it had justifiably derived from a place of unfortunate truth – if I knew deep within myself that I had much to atone for – much traction to gain and ground to cover – and especially, if the TICK TOCK CLOCK of cancer and prognosis was looming over me. I will never, ever understand how it is maternally possible for a woman especially, to walk out on her own children. How does one even attempt to live a life without their children and knowing it is by selfish, choice? How does one enjoy food, travel, or entertainment? (all these things my Mum loved and indulged in). How do you ever have a decent, quality night's sleep without being haunted every night of the images of your children's faces and voices? How do you ever truly function on a day-to-day basis knowing you have physically abandoned and emotionally-scarred your own flesh and blood? Not sure the depths of numbness one must travel to in order to bury this much of themselves. Seems counter-productive and counter-intuitive and far more work energetically, I would think to disconnect than to rise – it never goes away, even if you do.

I caught myself doing it again – falling back into the same old, non-serving, self-destructive thought processes, patterns, and unhealthy habits... that which was out of my control. Move on, Lisa. Let it go, Lisa. If I received a dollar for every-time I had to talk myself down and repeat these sentiments to myself – I would have been the youngest ever millionaire to walk the face of this planet. Carry on, Lisa.

LIVING FEARLESSLY DOWNLOAD

When I feel angry or confused by the actions of those I do not understand, that is an indicator that I have more work to do on myself – that I have stepped out of myself to place more emphasis on others as opposed to focusing on remaining devoted and dedicated to fixing, repairing, healing, understanding, and growing, that which, I do not necessarily like within myself. It starts with me. If my soul or my spirit feels repelled by the energies of another person's aura or energies, and instinctually and intuitively, I trust myself enough to recognize the signals as a sign to move on – that is all that is required. People show us what they want us to see for whatever their reasons. What they show one person may be completely different than what they choose to show, share or emit to another person. We are all energy. Trust your own instincts and intuition. Stay or move on. I have learnt not to unnecessarily complicate or to unnecessarily lengthen this process for myself. Swift and Simple. IT IS A CHOICE!

CHAPTER 10

'IN-TUITION' IS ALWAYS RIGHT

In 2002, I had been extended the invitation to join my Mum and step-father, and a few other couples who were friends of theirs, to my step-father's 40th birthday celebration in Corfu, Greece. This was a turning point, catalyst type year in my life and for many reasons. I had graduated as a mature student from McMaster University in Hamilton, Ontario, Canada. Like many things I chose to manifest in my life, I had to learn and develop my patience muscle, as doing most everything on my own, required the alignment of monies coupled with timing.

I was eventually able to afford my own university tuition and books, while also working full-time as a then, Live-In Manager for 3.5 years, where I lived and looked after four aged women who were differently-abled (my clients). Based upon the uniqueness of the position and it being a 24/7, 365 days a year, job within a residential setting, the agency I worked for provided me with 40 hours of additional staffing per week so as to receive a reprieve, and to alleviate the potential for burnout. It was a high needs, all-encompassing position. I had chosen to use my forty hours of staffing per week to earn my BA Degree in Sociology, as I truly loved school and learning, and was very much filling the void of academia in my life, upon graduating from college after earning and obtaining my three year diploma. I knew then that I was not done with post-secondary education.

Acquiring knowledge in one way or another (in addition to the school of hard knocks) was always a non-negotiable for me and will continue as such, until the day I take my last breath on this planet we call Earth. Against the advice of the University Guidance/HR Department, I opted to accelerate my course-load. I had maxed out what I could take each semester as a 'part-time' mature student. A part-time schedule/course-load generally implied – double the length of time it would normally take to obtain a degree if enrolled as a full-time student. What should have taken someone on average, six to eight years to complete before graduating as a part-time student; I somehow managed to complete it in four and a half years, while working full-time in a front-line, Senior Management position – while also being obligated to carry a work pager. Another example of MINDSET.

Toward the last few months of working in that exact position, and nearing the end of my degree program, I had also simultaneously been sought out to step-in as an Acting Manager at a Women's Shelter – Women and Children Fleeing Domestic Violence. A colleague and very close friend of mine, proposed a two week commitment of my time, until such time it could be determined whether the manager I was filling in for would be returning to her position. A two-week commitment had turned into two months, which had then led to a full-time job offer. During the juggle of all of these responsibilities and commitments, I had also been asked by the Executive Director of the agency of where I was a Live-In Manager, to spear-head an Adhoc Committee for the parents whose adult children with developmental disabilities were on extensive waiting lists for permanent residency in the model of home I was already working and living in with my clients. Each Live-In Manager was also required to provide a certain number of hours to these families for respite care within the Live-In home, which we individually managed.

Whenever I felt personally/professionally encumbered and over-extended in my own life, all I would have to do to switch my mindset, was change my focus, attention and energies on the women and children living communally within the shelter. Or the four clients of whom I looked after or the burnt-out, aged parents who were burning the candle at both ends with their own special needs children – often without a partner as they were widowed or who were grappling with their own chronic health issues and ongoing fatigue and the constant stressor of who was going to look after their adult special needs child once they themselves passed on. That was the only dose of perspective I required in order to carry on and carry on in a perpetual state of gratitude.

The Committee I was tasked to spear-head was named 'G.R.O.W.L.' – Growing Restless on the Waiting List. As previously cited, I worked very closely with provincial and federal government officials and members of Parliament to assist in the doing of what needed to be done. As a result of passion, collaboration, desperation, and also being asked to initiate Public Service Announcements and Petitions, coordinating meeting upon meeting, providing tours of the agency, and a unified commitment to this plight with the voices, hands, and energies of many – to reiterate, we received un-precedented funding to open up new homes, to get adults with disabilities off of the extensive waiting list, oversaw major retro-fits, staff training, salary enhancements and we also managed to have BILL 125 passed and legislated by Parliament – 'The Ontarians with Disabilities Act.'

I regularly reflect on pretty much every phase, stage and aspect of my life and often ask myself – questions not uncommonly asked of me by others as well, "How Do You Pull Everything Off?" "How Are You Able

To Do So Many Labor-Intensive, and Tiring Tasks, All At Once and Get Them Accomplished While Averting Burn-Out or a Breakdown?"

GOOD QUESTION!

Truthfully, the answer is quite simple. "When you love what you do and you do what you love, and in my case, when you are committed to paying-it-forward and being of service-to-others, and when you choose to become emotionally connected to your dreams, your passions, your purpose in life, and all that drives you at the core of who you authentically are – you become tapped into a burgeoning energy within you, which will magnetically pull you deeper and closer to all, which you are universally meant to align with." This, in my opinion, is choosing to LIVE FEARLESSLY!

I whole-heartedly believe this to be my truth, and I believe for what I have chosen to manifest in my life, coupled with the un-wavering core belief I have in myself, and my choosing to take massive action every single day of my life – I believe my life and how I choose to live it, is a testament to the old adage of, 'Anything Is Possible.' You truly do have to believe in yourself, love yourself, forgive yourself, and consistently work on yourself in order to deepen, grow, expand and evolve as a human being. Nothing changes if we individually do not change ourselves first and foremost and for the better and best. I am also an inherently grateful person. I have been reminded my entire life, largely in-part because of my lines of work, that there is always someone else who perceivably has it worse and would love to trade their problems and struggles in for mine. When one chooses to master these principles in one's own life, in one's own journey – beyond the sky is the limit. TRUTH! Everything extraordinary in life derives out of one's own attitude!

Therefore, in-spite of the ongoing instability in my relationship with my Mum, I was receptive to a much-needed reprieve and change of scenery. Off to Greece I flew. I stopped at my Grandma's in England for the night, before Greece and again, for another night following my trip to Greece and before returning home to Canada. Although it was my stepfather's birthday which brought me to this gathering it was customary for me to travel with gifts for my Mum as well. Again, I was always cognizant of her cancer and time. I was very selective in my gift purchasing and my gift giving with my Mum, specifically. I always elected to buy the sentimental type gifts and tear-jerker cards, forever hoping and wishing that the symbolism and heartfelt words would touch or reach a deeper cord within her and perhaps be the light-bulb, cathartic, catalyst push in the forward-facing step toward a positive, healing direction for us.

I was grateful to be sharing holiday space and energies with other people, even though I did not personally know them at the time of us all living communally in a villa. One of the women and I especially hit it off and almost immediately so. I found her to be extremely attentive, engaged and an immensely warm human being. She was the first person in my Mum's clan to have ever seemed genuinely interested in knowing the story/history of my relationship with my Mum, and not from an intrusive, gossipy, standpoint, but rather, from a place of legitimate confusion and concern. Without bombarding her with decades of drama, I had provided her enough details for her to understand the lay of the land and to supply her with just enough insight that, should anything go awry on this trip, she would be prepared and not overly shocked. This friend of my Mum and stepfather – oozed authentic compassion and an elevated sense of intuitiveness. She was a lovely breath of fresh air. I was immensely grateful to her for this unexpected infrastructure of support.

After my stepfather had opened all of his birthday gifts, my Mum had then proceeded to open up her carefully packaged bag of goodies from me. All was seemingly going well, until she un-wrapped the last and final gift from me – the one I had requested she open up last. My Mum had delicately peeled back the paper, opened up the box, and removed the statue from inside the box. I was so chuffed with myself. I loved the statue of mother and daughter embracing one another – part of the 'Willow' collection. My Mum, seemingly as touched by the statue as what I was, appeared to have been so deeply taken aback, that she broke down into what the rest of us believed to be as real hard and genuine tears. In that moment, my Mum's friend who was aware of some of our back-story, locked eyes with me; offering me such a beautiful smile, the kind that suggests you are deeply moved. It was an unspoken exchange between the two of us as if to say, "Well done, Lisa – such a beautiful and meaningful gift." I really clutched onto this moment – truly believed it was a gateway to a newfound beginning for my Mum and I. FINALLY!

Instantly, I was transported back to reality when what I thought was my Mum on the brink of springing forward, heartfelt tears, and my believing that she too was overcome with deeply felt emotion; quickly transformed into her laughing. It had clearly been an uncomfortable moment for her, especially with so many pairs of eyes gauging and anticipating her reaction, and so she had gone from pretending to cry to laughing, to then thanking me from across the table. My Mum's friend immediately looked at me, again. I could tell that her heart sank for me in that moment, as much as it had sunk for myself. I could not hold her gaze for too long, as my Mum's display of pretending to break out into tears was now just about to set my own into un-stoppable action.

Well, if nothing else, at least there was one person in my Mum's camp who caught a glimpse of the emotional cruelty and psychological bullshit, which was the story and fabric of my Mum and me. It was another deflating moment, but at least there was a remnant of vindication and validation for me for feeling as though my Mum had somewhat been 'found out' – exposed for the other mask worn by Jenny. At this point, I was willing to accept any consolation prize willing to be offered up. All in all, I suppose you could say that this trip had been one of the more successful visits shared by my Mum and I underneath the same roof, given I was not kicked out and prematurely put back on a plane. I was always looking for the bright light and upside in any given situation – you have to, as there always is one, no matter how small!

LIVING FEARLESSLY DOWNLOAD

No matter who the person or the relationship or your expectations of what you believe should be innately forthcoming, I have learnt and painfully so, that you cannot force connection. You cannot force another person to want to grow or expand or evolve. You cannot force individuals to want to go deep within themselves or do the internal work. One must arrive, if ever at all, to the time, place, and space of this becoming even possible if important enough to them to incorporate these practices and beliefs into their own lives. We are all operating at different levels of self-awareness. We are all wired differently. We all want for different 'things' in our lives. We are all catapulted into change at different times in our lives and for our own set of circumstances and reasons. As difficult or as confusing as it may be to understand why someone else may not wish to embrace you into their own lives or into their own hearts, you have to not only respect their decision for what it is but more importantly, you have to respect yourself enough to walk away. IT IS A CHOICE!

CHAPTER 11

DOUBLE WHAMMY

I landed back at my Grandma's in Essex, England – just the two of us on my last full day/night with her, before flying back to Canada. My Grandma and I walked together for a pub lunch in the village. Grandma of course wanted to know how my holiday in Corfu had gone. How her daughter appeared health wise, and so forth. I shared quite openly and honestly with her what had unfolded regarding the mother/daughter statue gift I had given to my Mum. My Grandma's facial response was not unlike that of my Mum's friend, who had seen the whole incident unfold firsthand. Grandma always tried to do her very best in whatever way she knew how, to try and find the right words to almost apologize for my Mum's insensitivities toward me. While tucking into our pub-lunch, I asked my Grandma if I could ask her a question. In fairness to her, I promised it as being a very difficult question to ask and an equally difficult one for her to answer.

She placed her fork and knife down on her plate and encouraged me to proceed with what I wanted and needed to know. "I need to know, Grandma, if both you and Mum were aware of Reg having been a pedophile?" "I need to know why no-one knowingly protected me if you and Mum were already aware that he was." Grandma looked at me with that sunken, weathered look I had unfortunately seen one too many times upon her sweet face. No matter the level of culpability my Grandma shared in the early events of my life, I loved her fiercely and unconditionally. She had had a very difficult life and I only know but mere fragments of it. I cannot even begin to imagine all the painstaking secrets never before shared with me. It was a badge of honor when people said that I reminded them of my Grandma, as there are many parallels shared between the two of us.

Grandma was a woman who started out as a nurse before becoming a teacher of children with special needs. Grandma was always extremely active in her community – always supporting one charitable cause after another. She was forever the person people had sought out for counsel and as a safe haven – the preferred shoulder to lean on. My spirit was deeply akin to that of my Grandma's. Having been born and raised on the family-owned Assam Tea Plantation in Shillong, India – her mother belonging to the Karsi Caste and her Dad, a Brit. When she and her family immigrated to England in her younger years, it was customary back then that those who chose to emigrate could not take their wealth with them. I remember my Grandma proudly sharing with me that she had smuggled an armful of bangles underneath all of her layered clothing for the flight to England, where she made her permanent home, until her death a few years ago. This was of course long before the airports advanced security systems and protocols had been instituted.

"Yes, Lisa. Your Mum and I both knew what Reg was and what he had done and not just to you, but to other members of the family including Angie." – Angie being my Grandma's other daughter and my Mum's only other sibling. I knew about Angie as she herself had personally told me during one of my hellish childhood summers spent in England.

"Did he abuse Mum as well?" "She told me that he had not when I had asked her the very same question years ago."

"I do not believe so. As far as I know, it only happened to Angie." "I am very sorry, Lisa. Your Mum and I both failed you miserably with all of that." "It never should have been allowed to happen. He never should have been allowed any proximity or access to you at all." "I know this is easy for me to say, after all these years have passed, and I know my apology changes nothing with any of it, dear. I won't make excuses to you other than to say; I had already had one previously failed marriage with your Grandfather Fred – whom you've only met a few times in your life. Divorce was taboo back in my day and the thought of going through it a second time was too unbearable for me. I have many horrible regrets in my life, Lisa – what has happened to you, to Angie and to many others, including his own daughters of his first marriage in New Zealand. What I have allowed to happen is unforgivable, I know. I was stuck and I was many a-time in a dark place in my life, Lisa. I am so terribly sorry and heart-sick."

I had already suspected that my Grandma knew. This was apparent to me during all the times of it being Reg, myself and my Grandma being in the same room together. She never hid her disdain and disgust for him when it was just me, present in their company. She was forever harshly nudging him with her elbow when she often caught him inappropriately gawking at me from across the room. She was never subtle of her deeply held resentment toward him when I was the only one to bear witness. He didn't care and nothing she did, said or gestured ever discouraged him because at the end of the day he was manipulative enough to know that he had received a free pass to basically do whatever he wanted and to whomever he wanted. He had never truly been held accountable by anyone and so he did what other pedophiles that are un-stopped do – he perpetually abused and violated innocent female children.

After all of these years, I was truthfully just grateful to have received my Grandma's willingness to participate in the discussion – to painfully hear me with an open heart – to know that I was at the very least, worthy and deserving of finally being told the truth. The apology was an added bonus and to finally learn what I had already strongly suspected all these years – that my Mum (and her) did in fact know of Reg's history – knew full well his tendencies, knew he was a pedophile. Intuitively, I think my younger self knew that my Mum had always known when I think back to the conversation she and I had on my bed, following her birthday celebration at her best friend's house – the one on the heels of Reg's hand having been in my crotch throughout it all. Something had resonated as 'off' when it was she NOT me who had said, "Did HE do something to you?" That was the disclosure and acknowledgement right there in a nutshell.

The dots were all finally beginning to connect. The pieces of the puzzle were all taking shape and fitting together, except for the one piece, which was never intended to fit I suppose – the WHY – the unknown of how my Mum could idly stand by and willingly choose to fail to protect her first born child. Funny isn't it – how the not knowing of the most negatively profound aspect of my life – one of the worst things imaginable to happen to an innocent child, can become the 'WHY' factor for how one bridges their deepest pain and transform it into their deepest passions, hence their intended purpose in life. NO COINCIDENCES!

Rather than brooding or dwelling or remaining stuck in the sphere of not being able to turn back the clock or my ever coming to understand as to the answer or reason or insights for the torturous unknowing of the 'WHY' – Instead, I chose to focus on what WAS in my perceivable control within this dilemma. I took from this, the gift of how I chose to interpret the unfairness associated with my Mum never giving me her, 'WHY.' Perhaps learning the 'WHY' would have altered every other aspect of my journey from that point forward. Perhaps learning the, 'WHY' would have haunted my soul, which might very well have altered my sanity, or shattered my soul or pierced my heart beyond any point of return, or plagued my mind beyond my capabilities of ever again being able to shift and reverse my mindset. Learning the 'WHY' might have actually unleashed a form of carnage I may not have been able to survive.

I sat deeply with myself in this stream of consciousness. Thoughts of my entire life had flooded through me and in chronological format. I allowed myself to sit with all the pain once and for all. Every single memory of what hurt me, I allowed myself to sit with it – to feel it all. I had too much at stake with my newfound path, to chance all this being for not by not allowing myself to feel this all now and all at once. Feel it now or feel it later and if later, it could have dire consequences on my future path of all that I endeavored to do with my life and what I endeavored to do was to reach the masses. It wasn't just me on the line it was all the nameless faces I had yet to cross paths with. Go deep, Lisa.

I mentally recalled every milestone my Mum was absent from – high school, college and university graduations. I recalled every death in my family, which I was never invited to attend and in some cases, even initially informed of – my maternal cousin, Christopher in England who had committed suicide. He was the son of my Aunt Angie – my Mum's sister and only sibling. Angie had also passed on, due to metastatic breast cancer – she like my Mum was also diagnosed at the age of forty-four. The passing of my Grandma, Molly. My Grandma's brother – my Uncle Peter, my Nana Jean in Scotland (my Dad's Mum) my Uncle Bill – my Dad's brother, also from Scotland, and eventually my Mum herself in 2014. Even in death my absence was not welcome for reasons previously cited to me by my Mum as it pertained to other family members who passed before her – reasons, which spoke to inconvenience of having to house me with a place to stay given all my Mum's side of the family were located in England. Even in death, my feelings or individual relationship to members of my family was negated, minimized, de-valued and ultimately, I felt as though I could have been buried alongside them for the lack of regard and compassion ever showed to me for my own sense of loss. I mentally downloaded it all – sat with it and simply sobbed.

LIVING FEARLESSLY DOWNLOAD

It is not important to focus your energies on those who have chosen not to show up in your life, but rather, it is more important that you choose to show up in your own life and be present for yourself. It is counter-intuitive to spend your time and energies chasing people for their affection, their approval, their love, and their acceptance of you. For whatever the block, the reason, the circumstance for someone not choosing to see in you what you most importantly must fundamentally see within yourself, is moot. When you externally require others to love you that is an indication that there is a lack of love you internally have for yourself. When you externally require others to approve of you, this is an indication that you do not internally believe you are already enough. Love yourself not just 'enough' – love yourself 'fully' so whenever you are faced with the prospect of anyone else outside of you, choosing to reject you, abandon you, alienate you, silence you, dismiss you and so on... it will not adversely or profoundly impact you to the point of imploding or sabotaging yourself by deeming yourself unworthy, undeserving or unloving a human being. This is false. Love yourself and move on! IT IS A CHOICE!

Chapter 12

TILL DEATH DO US PART

Interesting that the only milestone that genuinely got celebrated in my life was when my Mum got to enjoy the role of being mother-of-the-bride. It seemed to be the one and only event and time in my life, where my Mum felt most proud of me. My journey of embarking upon marriage seemed to have been synonymous with my finally 'Having Made It' or my choosing to 'Grow Up and Get With the Program' or my 'Having Come Into My Own' and evolving as a woman and as a human being.

My getting married took on the persona of mother and daughter bonding, as it was the only milestone (before becoming a mother/parent, myself) that we actually shared in common. Being relatable to one another with something she could personally identify with, (marriage) temporarily changed our status quo. Rather than listening to me dribble on about causes, client-case-load, policies, procedures or my experiences with academia (all uncomfortable and non-relatable subject matters for her) we instead, got to travel to the superficial world called wedding planning. My Mum was in her complete element with the light and fluffiness of menu-planning, cake-tasting, wedding-gown shopping, compiling lists for guests, flowers, photographers, music, and all the other hype one might imagine, that goes into the planning and organizing for only one day on the calendar.

Living out-west at this time of my life, my (then) soon-to-be husband and I both had set our intentions on an autumn wedding – our favorite season. We had wanted to get married in Jasper, Alberta, Canada – our favorite place to be and go once we had discovered it, together. We had ideally both wished for an outdoor wedding as we were/are both outdoor enthusiasts and nature junkies. We had every intention of paying for the wedding ourselves, and truthfully for me, that was instinctually already a no-brainer given I was already accustomed to paying my own way through life for everything, already, anyway.

One would think that if you were planning to pay for your own wedding, never mind the fact that the wedding itself symbolizes it being the special and unique day for two specific individuals – the ONE day that you should be able to exercise carte blanche with decision-making, choices and such, but alas…based on family dynamics and family history being what it was, this was not to be the case.

Due to climate changes, which went hand-in-hand with seasonal changes – the venue was switched from an autumn, outdoor, in-nature, Canadian Event to a spring, indoor, not in nature, church, United States Event. See where this is going? This of course became necessary so as to accommodate my Mum's health condition and health concerns and the never-not-knowingness of what might change or worsen in advance of anything previously scheduled. Go-Team! Wedding Enthusiasm got replaced with subject matters specific to the unknown of what my Mum's forecasted cocktail of meds and treatment regimen might be around the timing of the wedding. Would she receive medical clearance to travel by air? How much more compromised might her immune system be by then? Would she even still be alive? (Would any of us?)

Who was I to take issue and once again, what would that have said about me as a daughter, had I not conceded or put on the 'Mum and

Cancer Comes First' hat? Again, had my relationship with my Mum been a healthy, reciprocal, mutually respectful, loving, nurturing, give and take one – there would have been zero cringing or resentment on my part. I know who I am at the core of who I am. My heart is a loving heart. I have been selfless my whole life and much to my own detriment in some respects. I know that I genuinely possess goodness in my soul and readily, willingly and energetically, emit that spirit out into the universe. I truly would not have batted an eyelash where the changes to the wedding were concerned, had history been different.

Without making my Mum feel guilty or responsible for all of the changes to my wedding, I plodded onwards. Thinking that at the very least, my then soon-to-be-husband and I could be the ones to mutually decide upon the Spring Wedding date – we soon came to realize that our suggested preferences did not coincide with my step-father's business travelling itinerary and in addition to that we had another family member throw in her two cents for preferred dates so that she wouldn't encounter a scheduling conflict with a pre-booked trip to the Cayman Islands. Can you spell DONE?

To appease my Mum, while once again taking into account that this may be the one and only milestone event she would ever be able to cel-ebrate in her daughter's life, I let her have final approval and say on the dress, the cake, the church, the engagement party, the-everything, right down to my hairdo and jewelry. Rather than resisting her every step of the way (so as to preserve my own sanity and to not rob my fiancé of his right to happiness by seeing me chronically fuming) I handed it all off to my Mum. Her being the mother-of-the-bride was seemingly more important, than me being the bride and therefore, I chose to relinquish and surrender it all.

One of the more important reasons why I wished to have my spe-cial day in Canada was because of the closeness I share with my former step-mother/friend, Diana and my two half-siblings, Evan and Lauren. In-spite of an unfortunate estrangement, I then had with my Dad (due to wife number three – we'll leave it there) – my then soon-to-be-husband had still done the honorable thing by traditionally asking the father-of-the-bride for his blessing for his daughter's hand in marriage. My Dad was happy for us and had offered his blessing, although, when due to awkwardness surrounding my hoping and wanting for both my Dad and step-father to walk me down the wedding-aisle – especially given the logistics surrounding the wedding venue being moved to the states where my Mum and step-father lived, things sadly and unfortunately digressed and only one person ended up walking me down the aisle or was even in attendance on my special day – my step-father.

For whatever the reason, when I was close to my Dad, things were 'off' between my Mum and me and when I was perceivably 'on' again with my Mum, the relationship with my Dad (and for other factors, too) felt strained. There were too many extenuating circumstances, logistical factors, unhealed relationships, and awkward dynamics at that particular time, which disallowed the entire inclusion of my family – immediate, extended and blended. Interesting that children generally have to accept whatever decisions their parents make with respect to divorce, re-marriage, step-parents, half-siblings, step-siblings and put on the happy face no matter how it stands to affect and impact the rest of their lives, but when an adult child asks the adults to put on the happy face for only one day – HER special day – it becomes the biggest shit-show one might imagine. Let It Go, Lisa! Carry On!

LIVING FEARLESSLY DOWNLOAD

Relationships and partnerships only healthily grow, blossom and flourish and result in what one would deem to be 'successful' to the degree where each individual person is committed to watering, feeding and nurturing their own soul. When two people are equally and mutually committed to loving themselves first, recognizing, admitting, and atoning for their own short-comings, inadequacies, first – when two people are equally and mutually committed to honing themselves and upping their own game, standards and boundaries, then you will attract that in another person. You will recognize, respect and appreciate that same level of fierce commitment to self in another because you are in-tune with yourself to know that you authentically are seeking and attracting the same. We often short-change our own growth and development and do not recognize it as such until we find ourselves in the same histrionic patterns of so called failed-relationships. When we have not developed or honed our self-love muscle, we subconsciously seek out people to fill our lives, fill our voids thinking that is the answer or the solution to making ourselves whole again and when we find ourselves repeating our own histories, telling ourselves the same stories, chasing the wrong things, and until we do the much needed internal work, we will continue to convince ourselves and others, that it was someone else's fault. Choose better by choosing to improve yourself first. IT IS A CHOICE!

CHAPTER 13

A SEASON, A REASON, A LIFETIME

My Mum was still with us when I became pregnant for the first time. I was married in May of 2007 and my beautiful son was born in September of 2008. When I had surpassed that first trimester of my pregnancy, it was then I had initiated the discussion with my Mum of my wanting and wishing to give her the honor and the privilege of being by my side in the delivery room. I really, in-truly believed that for my Mum to experience her own daughter giving birth to her own child, and she bearing witness to that miracle, HAD TO BE the defining, pivotal, cathartic, bonding, healing moment for the two of us. I was convinced of that with every fiber of my being.

I vividly remember the long-distance telephone conversation I had played over in my mind, quite a few times, before actually dialing my Mum's number and hearing her voice on the receiving end. I had conjured up this image in my mind that upon her hearing me say the words of my wanting her beside me in the delivery room, to witness the birth of her first grandchild, that she would automatically be reduced to a puddle of joy-filled tears – that she would express heartfelt gratitude of being deeply touched and honored by my request and would tell me that she would not miss this once in a lifetime first that any mother and daughter could be so fortunate to share in together, especially in her circumstance of having metastatic breast cancer. Every additional year that she was blessed to have received the gift of an extra year was conversely, also a subtle reminder (as we were all cognizant of) she was perhaps running on borrowed time and that the opportunity to celebrate in such significant milestone moments together, was winding down.

My Mum held the world record for being the only person in my life who ever seemed to have the capability of taking me from one extreme emotionally, to the other end of the spectrum, in zero seconds flat. I suppose I anticipated the 'Mother' of all reactions (pun intended) and one I had hoped to work in my favor – just once before she departed this Mother-Earth. By comparison, I could not conceive of any other event or milestone, or precious miracle-moment, that a parent – soon to be grandparent, would choose to voluntarily miss out on. For everything she and I had gone through, I thought she would have jumped all over it. Silly Lisa. Without any pause for consideration or contemplation, the minute my request escaped my mouth, I was met with, "I don't think that will work Lisa, as Tom and I are hoping to go away on vacation around that same time."

"Oh," was all I could muster. She filled in the awkward silence, while detecting, but not addressing, my noticeable hurt and disappointment.

"Have you guys booked your airline tickets yet?" I sheepishly asked.

"No, not as of yet, but the timing of your delivery date is approximately the same time frame we had previously discussed our going away, as it is what best fits with Tom's work/travel schedule. We'll come see you sometime after you've all had time to settle in with the baby and adjust. We can talk closer to the time of when that might be best for everyone's schedules."

"Okay, Mum. Talk soon. Bye."

Here I was again always trying to find the bright light, the gift, the message, the lesson in every situation no matter how gut wrenching, deflating, or dim. In order to once again plod on with one foot in front of the other, I continued as I always have – to self-dialogue. "That moment will come, Lisa. When she gets here and sees you with your own child – her grandchild in my arms." "It will be different then." I had to believe this. I had to convince myself of this to get through it all and keep my energies positive for my un-born baby.

LIVING FEARLESSLY DOWNLOAD

When we learn to become more than enough for ourselves, when we can reach that pinnacle of, "I am going to be perfectly fine, no matter what," anything else additionally just becomes an added bonus. People who healthily show up are an added bonus. People who healthily show up and who healthily stay - are an added bonus. People who unhealthily show up and who healthily leave, is an added bonus. If you are intrinsically strong and sound within yourself, (have to develop these muscles) you will consistently and easily reach that pinnacle of 'I am going to be more than fine, no matter what.' Being more than comfortable in your own skin is always more important than being less of who you authentically are in the presence of anyone else. Less is more. Choosing to honor you first and foremost is always a choice toward choosing wisely! IT IS A CHOICE!

Chapter 14

ONE TOO MANY ICE-CREAM CONES

My Mum had the opportunity to see me pregnant. Not sure if she felt badly about the fact she was planning on being on vacation at the timing of my delivery date and that prompting her to invite me to Virginia to spend one on one time together or not. However, I accepted her invitation, nonetheless. Maybe seeing me pregnant would speed up the outcome of what I was hoping to see come to fruition between she and I within our relationship. I was cautiously optimistic and for the sake of my un-born baby, my emphasis energetically was more centered on optimism than cynicism.

My Mum proudly showed me off to her friends and had kindly thrown me a couple of baby showers inclusive of different circles of her friends. I was genuinely touched and I knew it was a special moment for my Mum. She was in her comfort zone being with those she did not share history with, especially as it pertained to our true mother/daughter relationship. It would have been a different dynamic if it were baby showers inclusive of her and my friends and other family members in Canada – so I sensed her relief that she could do what soon-to-be-grandmothers do for their expectant daughters, without having to contend with some of the strife, similar to what surrounded my wedding only one year beforehand.

It was striking to me, the polarities, which differentiated us from one another – right down to the defining moments and circumstances, which catapulted us into our individualized 'Reinvention Processes.' Outside of much of our time together being spent amongst other people, two one-on-one moments shared between me and my Mum on this trip, had sent the pendulum swinging once again with two very interconnected exchanges between us.

It was exceptionally hot in Virginia during my visit. My Mum had suggested we go to her favorite ice-cream haunt, which happened to be in the same strip-mall plaza as a Baby Accessory-Gift Store. I thoroughly relished and hungrily lapped up this one on one time I was spending with my Mum. I loved and appreciated our leisurely strolls to wherever she wished to navigate me. So far, so good!

After our baby store gallivanting and enjoyment of ice-cream together, we had decided to call it a day and return to her AC'D home, and get me off my swollen feet. My protruding belly was starting to slow me down, coupled with all the walking and the scorching heat. Sometime after we had polished off our ice-cream cones, my Mum kept the food coming my way – all good, healthy and nutritious. I had always been a grazer type eater and so I welcomed the strawberries and the yoghurt, the crackers and the cheese, all the yumminess she had continually prepared and offered me. I wanted to keep her happy and do whatever I could to ensure she felt appreciated for all of her efforts and gestures of kindness toward me. After I had gratefully devoured all the small plates of food prepared for me, my Mum looked at me and out of the blue, had randomly made a comment to me that stung like hell.

"You really should watch how much you eat, Lisa. You still have a few months left and you already look as though you could go any day now." I excused myself to go to the bathroom where I blasted both the hot and cold sink faucets, while quietly sobbing on the floor for about ten minutes. I was grateful to hear her on the phone when I re-emerged from the bathroom. She had the television on in the living room, while she continued with her phone call conversation in the sunroom. No coincidences. The one person who always seemed to 'show up' for me in my periods of darkness – who seemed to always be speaking directly to me – more importantly – to my heart was my intangible mentor – Oprah Winfrey. I had purposely sunk myself down into a sideways lying position on the couch with a blanket (AC was cranked) pulled up to underneath my chin. I didn't want to draw attention to the fact that my eyes were still a bit red and puffy.

My Mum sat in her usual corner chair opposite me in the spaciously sized living room, so I was able to conceal myself quite well, while focusing on Oprah on the television. My Mum, was now off the phone, and was equally and intently watching alongside me, while she crocheted a lap blanket for some unknown person. Again, no coincidences. This particular segment of Oprah had to do with children of various ages, disclosing stories and details of events that had unfolded in their lives, which left lingering repercussions on their self-esteem, self-confidence and sense of self as people trying to overcome their emotional scars. WOW! Could not believe that of all show topics to be aired, Oprah was covering this subject matter specifically, and on a day that both my Mum and I would be watching together.

I will never forget what one of the female, teen guests had said with regards to what she grappled with in her story. She spoke of how she and her siblings had primarily been raised by their Dad, after her Mum had experienced either some form of depression or a breakdown and had walked out on her, her brothers, sisters and her Dad and had gone on to say that it had been the worst time in her life. She spoke of how she always felt as though she herself personally, was somehow responsible for her Mum feeling the need to get away from her and her family. She spoke of how this had resulted in her own cycle of depressive moments in her life followed up by self-loathing, self-loathing behaviors and thought patterns. If memory serves me correctly, I believe she may have even shared this tragic event of abandonment, morphing into a full-scale eating disorder, although, I cannot say for absolute sure. This sad girl went on to say that she then transformed into a wannabe self-perfectionist – over-achieving and over-excelling at everything she did – convincing herself that if she was 'Good Enough,' 'Behaved Enough' that maybe her Mum would decide to return home to she and her family.

This girls very vulnerable and public display of pain and bravery, completely, one hundred percent, resonated with me in the deepest core of my being. I was already feeling emotionally unhinged, I was pregnant, hormonal and hurt by my Mum's words. The combination threw me for a loop and I could no longer control the floodgates. I very quietly, while buried underneath the blanket, just let the tears uncontrollably stream down my face, while continuing to sit in silence with my Mum; watching what could be our story unfolding before the two of us, on the screen in my Mum's living room. After the show ended and had automatically switched over to local news, my Mum went and busied herself with the dishwasher in the kitchen. I called out from the living room, wishing her a good night, saying I was off to bed to read before going to sleep early. I think we were both grateful for deciding to call it a day.

I found myself feeling self-conscious at the table the next morning, when trying to find the appropriate answer to the question of what I wished to eat for breakfast. Putting my now heightened sensitivities of food consumption aside, I was of course and as I should be, primarily concerned and cognizant of the baby's nutritional needs coming before my own emotional fragilities or any other potential egg-shell type moment possibly erupting between my Mum and I.

While my Mum placed rye toast and marmalade in front of me, she started to speak with a wavering crackle in her voice. I recognized it instantly. That is how my voice would also sound when I was trying desperately not to cry while talking. "Lisa, I was up most of last night crying. I am sorry for what I said to you, yesterday. What I said was wrong and it is important that you feel comfortable eating, especially while you are pregnant and eating for two." Even though that was all my Mum could muster to say to me, I know that her extended apology encompassed other things, which remained un-spoken between us. I could tell the Oprah show had hit her hard. In my heart of hearts, I also know that Oprah was ultimately responsible for this breakthrough moment between us. The fact that this was transpiring over us breaking bread, added to the humor-infused irony of it all. Not to mention, everyone knows how much Oprah loves her bread. Thank you, Mum. Thank you, Oprah.

LIVING FEARLESSLY DOWNLOAD

Even in the moments of feeling as though we are perceivably treated as less than based on how others may choose to interact with us or engage us – there is however, an invaluable lesson to be learned. Rather than us focusing our energies on those who have perceivably been mean spirited or unfair – we can instead choose to focus our attention and energies back to the place of gratitude. These energetic reminders of what insult our souls and spirits is a positive reaffirmation of the boundaries and standards we are to establish and uphold for ourselves. Holding true to who you are authentically helps to also dismantle the cycle of unnecessary pain and needless suffering. Recognize the gift. Embrace the lesson. IT IS A CHOICE!

CHAPTER 15

I ALMOST DIED, TODAY

I was blessed with a beautiful pregnancy. Every medical check-up and ultra-sound, thankfully produced positive results and outcomes. I had not encountered any of the known challenges often associated with pregnancy, such as morning sickness, back-pain, food aversions or anything of the like. I never took for granted how fortunate I was for having such a smooth-sailing pregnancy from beginning to...

My husband and I had been invited to his Aunt and Uncle's home for dinner one evening – around the same timeframe of one of my ball-parked due dates (I had received a few; although, all close to one another). I had no family of my own out-west, but was grateful for the few members on my husband's side, who also lived in the same province as us. We had all just finished devouring my favorite meal of salmon and vegetables. Little did I know at the time that that would be my last meal for well over twenty-four hours and at one point, quite nearly my last ever-meal. I had offered to help clear the table and do the dishes, but had first excused myself to go to the washroom.

Everything felt and appeared normal, until I went to wipe myself after urinating. It was then that I became aware of the blood – I was excessively bleeding. Surprisingly, I was unbelievably calm. I wiped myself with nonstop handfuls of toilet paper before it became clear to me that I had a real problem. The bleeding would not stop. I began fishing around underneath the bathroom counter, hoping to find sanitary pads; knowing however, that my husband's aunt was post-menopausal. I did a mach-speed look and came up empty. I stuffed my underwear with mounds of toilet paper, flushed the pure red, blood-filled toilet, skipped washing my hands and quickly opened the door. They were all two feet away from the bathroom in the adjacent room, looking at pictures on the computer. They all looked at me, knowing I had been in the bathroom for what seemed like an extended amount of time.

"I have to go to the hospital. I can't stop bleeding." Everyone went into organized panic mode. Betty, Mike's Aunt, started scurrying around looking for sanitary napkins as well. I honestly cannot remember whether or not she was able to locate one, before Mike and I rushed out the door to the car – first to drop off his visiting sister at our house, which was located two minutes away from the hospital, however, our home and the hospital was approximately twenty minutes away from where we currently were. Mike unlocked the door for his sister, quickly grabbing the already prepared diaper bag and off we raced to the St. Albert Hospital in AB.

I was immediately rushed through to an observation room to answer questions and show the amount of blood that had accumulated on the stuffed toilet paper from the timing of leaving Edmonton to arriving at the hospital. Fortunately, the bleeding had started to dissipate, however, the decision was made that I was going to be admitted. I remember there being a variety of nurses that evening and all of them mentioning it being a packed house for women going into labor. I remember some of the details of my experience in hospital, but not all.

I remember requesting and receiving an epidural. I remember graduating to excruciating levels of physical pain and many hours having passed before my son was officially born. I remember receiving the maximum allowable amounts of nitrous gas. I remember being told that my baby was in the posterior position. I remember being told that if I was not fully dilated by 8:00pm (the next evening) that I would have to be induced. I had never known such physical pain in my life – it truly is indescribable, even with my enduring it for hours on end. The nurses and the doctors were hopping like mad – the ward and beds were packed full and every woman on that floor knew that the medical staff was running off their feet to individually keep up with all of us. Eight o'clock came and went and still no doctor to provide me with the updated status of how many centimeters dilated I was or whether or not we had to proceed with or forego my needing to be induced.

Finally at 10:00pm that night, two hours after I was to have been informed of my status, I was told that I in-fact was ten centimeters fully dilated. Had the nurse checked in on me at 8:00pm, I would have been induced. No coincidences and once again, very grateful. I was medicated to the hilt and yet, still felt every level of inconceivable pain and discomfort as if I had received zero medical intervention. The doctors were somewhat concerned about that, but we all marched on doing what was individually required of us in our differing roles.

My half lucid brain raced to every imaginable place possible. I tried desperately to shift my mindset away from the thoughts, which began to occupy all recesses of my mind. I began questioning myself. Was this happening to me because of the stress and emotional grief I experienced only a brief two months beforehand? Following a one-on-one lunch I had had with Mike's Uncle at my house in the backyard on a weekday, the two of us had somehow wound up on the subject of life and death. It was a very thoughtful and insightful discussion we had shared. After thanking him for his company and seeing him off at the door, I ventured upstairs to my computer to check on my emails, while the conversation of life and death and perspectives related to it still lingered with me.

I saw the number of emails in my inbox and immediately went to the one from my close friend, Laura, first. I opened it up only to realize that Laura was not the sender of the email. It was from her eldest daughter, Shannon, writing to me off of the last email exchange between her Mum and I.

'Lisa, its Shannon. Emergency. Call home ASAP.'

I intuitively knew what the news was going to be, but chose not to let my mind go there, until I first talked to Shannon. I had only talked to Laura by phone, the week prior. It was in that lengthy discussion that Laura had told me of her intentions to shop around for flights for she and the two girls to come out-west after the baby had been born. Her girls were at that age where they would want to hit up the West Edmonton Mall. Laura had been the one to make specific mention of this to me. We had got each other caught up on our individual lives, which years prior, had held simultaneous realities for the two of us as we had both been Managers of adolescent group homes for the same agency. She ran one house and I ran another. We had initially met at agency meetings and work related gatherings and then instantly became friends – seeing each other on a fairly regular basis, became confidants to one another – truly tight we were. Our worlds could not be more different now, but that fact and anything else combined, had never altered our deep love for one another, our sisterly bond. The growing polarities of our individual lives only served to make for better and more interesting conversation from two different perspectives of women who had already established a sol-id foundation, rooted in kindred-souls. We always had each other's best interest at heart – never any pressure or drama no matter how busy life got or the challenge of living in two separate provinces or time zones. We picked up wherever we left off with truly deep connection and loving energy. I was grateful to Laura for being that kind of a friend and for having such a beautiful demeanor and disposition. Laura and I had ended that last telephone conversation with the promise that we would speak the following week on the same evening and at the same time.

That phone call or any other phone call from Laura would never again materialize. I dialed Laura's telephone number and instantly, Shannon picked up. Shannon very calmly and matter-of-factly, provided me with the details surrounding the news of Laura's suicide. I was completely gutted. Gutted and back up to the four corners of the ceiling I went.

It was unfortunately not advisable for me to return to Ontario for Laura's service, given how far along I was into my pregnancy and the emotional anguish I was grappling with. Mike was reserving his time off of work for when the baby came and he did not want me travelling alone under these circumstances. I felt horribly conflicted by this dilemma as my pain and loss could never compare to Laura's two daughters, who I so desperately wanted to be present for and to provide comfort to, especially during this darkest time in both of their lives. I found little consolation in emailing the family my Eulogy and sending the customary flowers. Laura and her girls deserved more than that from me, particularly because of the unique and rare bond we had shared. We were family.

This all raced through my mind, while lying in sheer agony in the hospital bed wondering what was going on with my un-born child and me.

I remember on cue – pushing and breathing – pushing and breathing. The delivering doctor, Dr. Lidkea, was having a hell of a time with the baby and me especially with 'him' lying in a posterior position. The forceps had to come out. Finally, after eighteen hours, my son entered this world! I remember the umbilical cord being cut, I remember him being placed upon my chest. I remember him being measured, weighed, bathed and wrapped up. I remember Mike stepping outside the room…to make phone calls to both sets of parents. Then, I remember the delivering doctor, mounting me on the bed with her own body – going full-fisted inside of me. I remember being surrounded at my bedside by medical masks, hovering over me and beside me. I remember the same anesthesiologist who provided the epidural, now being right back at my side – injecting more fluids into my catheter. I will never forget the look on his face as he peered down on my fading eyes. I remember him squeezing my hand with both of his, whilst quietly mouthing a prayer underneath his breath. I remember a nurse standing directly behind me whose face I could see above mine. She was lovingly stroking my hair, and then I heard a variety of voices all chiming the same message to me, "Stay with us, Lisa. Stay with me. You have a beautiful baby boy who needs you. Stay with us, Lisa."

I was present and then I wasn't. I was aware and then I wasn't. I was in my body and then I wasn't. I was on the bed and then I was back on the ceiling, floating around, seeing myself, and watching myself, but not clearly. Everything was zoomed out and hazy. Everything appeared to be growing further and further out of focus and morphing into an accelerated distance. Was this the drugs? Was I hallucinating? Was I here? Was I gone? What was this? What was happening to me? Would I know if I was okay? Was I asleep? Was this a dream? Are these doctors really here? Are these people talking to me? I felt safe. I felt physically fine. I felt a warmth come over me. I felt at peace.

Perhaps because of all the drugs, perhaps because I knew my son had safely and healthily been born, I was in no state of panic. I sensed other people's panic, but I felt good. Confused when I was 'present,' –at peace when I was slipping. When whatever this was, subsided, I remember being told after imminent danger had passed (was not even aware that I had been in imminent danger) and in Mike's words, "That my hospital room resembled that of a murder scene." While he had been outside of my room placing phone calls to share our amazing news of the birth of our beautiful son, he was stopped in his tracks when he heard STAT blared over the loud speaker with my room number attached to the STAT alert. He then immediately, witnessed a barrage of medical personnel flying into my room, and walked in on seeing a hospital employee mopping up copious amounts of my blood all over the floor at the foot of my bedside. Then, eyeing the back of the delivering doctor perched upon me pulling, what we later came to learn was retained placenta, from deep inside of me. Mike later shared with me that when he had a split second to get the doctor's attention to ask her what was happening to me, she had quickly responded with, "Retained Placenta. She's hemorrhaging."

"Is she going to be okay?"

"It's looking grave at the moment. Doing everything we can."

I will never begin to fathom how horrific this entire ordeal must have been for Mike. He had already been riding an exhaustive roller-coaster pendulum from the time we initially rushed to the hospital because of my bleeding, to witnessing me being in ongoing excruciating pain, learning that our baby was in a posterior position, the understandable busyness of the doctors not being able to provide him with timely updates, to forceps, to the once-in-a-lifetime experience of seeing your first ever child being born, cutting the umbilical cord, making elated and relieved type telephone calls, to seeing your wife in the throes of death. I cannot even imagine. I will always feel for him for having to endure this ordeal and without having had the tangible family support and comfort readily made available to him.

I had come very close to almost requiring a mandatory blood transfusion, given the amount of blood loss I had suffered. The doctor and I had talked about the pros/cons, risks/benefits of voluntarily proceeding with receiving one. I am not completely sure I fully comprehended the entire conversation or all the information I was told. I truly was not up to par as far as processing details or mentally weighing or computing statistics. What I knew for sure was that I only wanted to be with my newborn son and get us all back home as soon as possible. The only conversation I was interested in entertaining, was one that included signing hospital discharge documents, especially after arriving at the definitive answer of a resounding NO for proceeding with a blood transfusion. To my way of thinking, although admittedly, my ability to think was skewed, discharge papers should naturally be the next order of business.

"Sorry, Lisa – you and your son cannot leave the hospital, at least not for the next couple of days. We are moving you to another private room in a different ward of the hospital. Because of your hemorrhage, your son is extremely jaundiced and requires incubated light-therapy. Because of your hemorrhage, you are extremely anemic and need to be temporarily monitored. Because of your hemorrhage, you are not expressing breast milk, which your son will healthily require for necessary growth and nourishment." I was crushed. Crushed that this was his beginning in life, and also, equally grateful that he at least had me, his Mummy, alive. We WOULD get through this as I did with every other perceivable crises or hardship in my life. I was a spirit-warrior so naturally, so was my son.

Once I reconciled the fact that it was not our time to depart the hospital, I switched my mindset, and began to channel all my thoughts and energies to it being my time and place to fight my son and I back to good health. That I could do. That I would do. However, that doesn't negate the fact of how emotionally distraught I felt catching my first glimpse of seeing my innocent baby all by himself in the light-therapy incubator, once my personal belongings were packed up and taken to our new room where he was already waiting for me. There was a circular opening for me to bottle feed him with my hand. After he had received initial amounts of required light-therapy, I remember the wave of gratitude and relief that washed over me when I was able to finally hold him, again and change his diaper for the first time. I had been encouraged by the medical staff to rest in the bed while he grew stronger in the incubator. I found that to be too much of an unfair and non-instinctual challenge and so I instead, spent most of my time sitting upright in an uncomfortable hospital chair, which I positioned as closely as I could to my son who was laying in this incubator. I talked to him, and loved him up fiercely regardless of the plastic barrier separating he and I physically. I sat with an extended arm for as long as I could withstand the discomfort of gravity – with him curling his finger around mine through the feeding-hole.

I had received a prescription for a year's worth of iron pills. Days after my son and I had been officially released from the hospital, I had received home visits from lactation therapists who tried working with me to successfully produce and express my breast milk. I was adamant that I was going to breast-feed my child. I had received a prescription for Domperidone, which helped alleviate this roadblock for me. There were many back and forth trips to a different hospital, than the one I had given birth in so as to have my son and I regularly monitored with the breastfeeding regimen and to monitor his ongoing growth and development. We had to chart mandatory three-hour input/output feedings to raise his percentiles. All this, while being continuously anemic, white as a ghost, and challenged by vertigo and sleep deprivation. A mother always does what a mother has to do!

It was a long road back to recovery for the two of us, but we did it and we triumphed as warriors, together – as Mother and Son. Always makes me emotional when I reflect upon those times. However, I choose to mentally and emotionally travel back in time to those days every once in a while, as it always lends perspective to how grateful I am. How fortunate I am. How blessed I am. And as a reminder to self during the ongoing challenges of life that present themselves and surface – I am reminded once more that I really can overcome anything I set my mind to and rise...if I choose to. I believe my son has subconsciously also acquired this same life lesson and mindset as a result of the resiliency and perseverance of his own old-soul, spirit.

LIVING FEARLESSLY DOWNLOAD

Often times we appreciate far more, the gifts and blessings of what we have when we have either lost our gifts or have been faced with the near possibility of losing them. I view this life lesson as universal wake-up calls. I can honestly say that I am authentically grateful for life, more specifically - the gift of my life, because I came close to losing my life (within this realm of existence). Although, I would like to believe that my own life experiences, coupled with having worked closely within crisis management with vulnerable populations of people being more than enough reason for my inherent gratitude – my near-death experience served to intensify, magnify, enrich the depths of my wholehearted gratitude. It offered me a uniquely rare insight and additional clarity of honing my ability to put things into so-called perspective. I think this became even more so pronounced, given the extenuating circumstances surrounding this event. Not to negate the relevance or significance of anyone else's near-death experiences, but I believe almost dying right after you have just given birth to a baby – having brought life into this world is about as profound a life lesson as one can universally receive with respect to distinguishing very quickly in one's own life – what matters and what does not. What carries currency and what does not. What holds value and what does not. As deep and as grateful a person as I characterize myself to be even back then and pre-near-death experience, it was mirrored back to me very clearly, the ways in-which I was still being trivial or not as fully grateful as I ought to be and as fully grateful as I had the potential to be. IT IS A CHOICE!

Chapter 16

GRANDMA ARRIVES

Eventually and when the climate and circumstances suited – my Mum came to visit her first grandchild and supported me through my ongoing challenges with anemia, vertigo and sleep deprivation. Thank goodness post-partum was not part of that equation. Mum was very kind and helpful with preparing batches of home-cooked lentil dishes and other nutritiously homemade meals to freeze for us long after her visit would come to an end. I was immensely grateful to her for that as it was one less thing I had to concern myself with. She was also extremely generous with all the purchased baby-gifts from her travels abroad, as well as the labor of love that went into the crocheted blankets and knitted sweaters she had made for my son. From that perspective, she really wore the stereotypical Grandma role, beautifully.

I had every reason to believe that this would be an incredible bonding experience for the two of us. After all, who does not feel more plugged-in, connected, warm and fuzzy, than a grandparent in the presence of their firstborn child, mothering their firstborn child? Had my Mum bore witness and experienced firsthand, the initial beginnings of what my son and I had gotten off to – perhaps that level of up-close-and-personal insight may have alleviated some of the tension, which shortly began to once again, rear its head. Knowing my Mum as well as I did – I had become an expert at reading her body language and non-verbal communication, better than I ever did her spoken word. Unfortunately, I had learnt and adapted this skill at the inappropriate age of four years old. Because of the trauma surrounding forceps, posterior position, jaundice, incubation, light-therapy, delayed breast-feeding, and likely sensing his Mum had been in danger, it goes without saying, why my son was not the best sleeper.

He would cry and I would immediately respond each and every time. I did this instinctually, intuitively, maternally and lovingly. My choosing to do so was met with disapproving glances each time I abruptly hopped out of a conversation that was mid-sentence, and dashed up to my son's nursery. I had also found it particularly interesting when my Mum would choose to in-directly talk to me through her conversations with the baby, as opposed to sharing with me directly and voluntarily, head-on, how she differed from myself in our approaches to mothering. I learnt all this through her body language and in her sideline conversations to my child, purposely within hearing proximity to me.

On a separate occasion, and on one my first times leaving my son at home, my Mum and I had ventured to a coffee shop for a couple of hours, after first pumping enough milk for my son's next feeding time in the event of us running a bit behind schedule. We paid for our coffees and settled into cozy lounge chairs, sitting directly opposite one another, face-to-face. While sipping on my decaf, my Mum wasted little time opening up Pandora's Box, which by the end of our time together, had left me reeling for many months after the fact. If not capable of having a positively, meaningful conversation, or at least a valiant attempt to have one, my second preference would have been to engage in light-hearted and superficial dialogue, given my still current state of health. Instead, I got hit with her choice of what hid behind door number three.

For whatever the reasoning or for why-ever the timing, my Mum proceeded to tell me that when it had become evident to her that her marriage to my Dad was approaching an irreconcilable, official parting of the ways, that she had felt and had become suicidal. She elaborated by going on to say that the only factor that prevented her from carrying it out, were the thoughts of leaving me and my brother behind. "And because I grappled with not wanting to live anymore, but also having the internal conflict of leaving you both behind, without me – I had decided to take all three of our lives, together. I had all the pills lined up and in my mind; we would all swallow the pills at the same time, while your Dad was out at one of his soccer games."

I sat speechless, looking at her, feeling completely dumbfounded, mortified, and numb all at once. My mind raced with simultaneous thoughts, images, and questions. My heart pulsated out of my body at the mere thought of my own child being left motherless, which had come very close to happening (involuntarily, I might add), but then stretching the darkness of my own thoughts to that of murdering my own child. WHAT? I completely downward spiraled in that moment.

My Mum was working with the knowledge that one of my closest and dearest of friends had just recently committed suicide; leaving behind two brokenhearted children, and as a single parent herself. She also knew that I had almost died on the delivery table; post childbirth. She also knew this had all un-raveled without her being by my side for any of it, given the priority being that of her vacation. She also knew that even while I sat here trying to absorb and process what she had just dumped on my lap, that I was still not one hundred percent fully recovered from the side effects of the massive hemorrhage, which almost claimed my life. She also knew that in-spite of all of these upheavals; I had endured in succession of one another, that I was committed to focusing on this still being what should be permitted for me to enjoy as – the happiest, most joy-filled, precious, and sacred time in my life. I was completely out of my depth and breadth for understanding her in this particular moment. The ability to assume a devil's advocate perspective, one I am usually exceptionally good at, was nowhere to be found.

Was I perhaps receiving too much attention? My hemorrhage/near death experience and a newborn child to boot – was this taking Mum out of the limelight? Were we not dedicating enough time, attention, focus and energies to her Cancer? Was this too much about Lisa and not enough about Jenny? Why, after what I had battled with and was residually still going through, why, for everything she and I had gone through together during our sordid relationship history, and why, with her knowing me well enough to know that I was more concentrated and committed to remaining positive, grateful, optimistic, healthy, and energized – why on earth would she of all times, choose to want to hurt me this way, during what was supposed to be the most special time in my life? I slipped again – was back on the why's of things that were not serving me and were only proving to weigh me down – plunging into the abyss of operating at my lowest vibrational level. I was now upset with myself, as much as I was upset with her, for I was doing the psychological dance, yet again.

Albeit a new mother, I was now a mother nonetheless. The only barometer I needed to use to measure a perceivable right from a perceivable wrong, were my own maternal instincts. My maternal instincts automatically swung my compass in the direction toward understanding how pronounced the polarities were between my Mum and I. This exchange cemented that for me. We could not have been more juxtaposed as women, as mothers, or as human beings altogether. Somewhere along the way, within my Mum's own journey, and for core reasons unbeknownst to me, she developed a massive disconnect from herself, never mind from me. Call it a coping mechanism, a survival instinct, call it mental health issues, a break from reality, a damaged or fractured sense of self-identity – whichever coined term one wishes to use, to perhaps describe this long-standing history of patterns, behaviors, traits, tendencies, and even if not completely obvious or apparent to anyone else other than me – that jaunt to the coffee shop with my Mum crystallized newfound understanding of all the why's I had questioned throughout the course of my entire life. I finally got it the more I mothered my own child.

Everything, which had plagued me – haunted me had in fact been explained to me in what I had been told over mother-daughter coffee-time. After the initial shock had worn off – the more I fell in love with my own child every single second – the more clarity I did in fact receive. Her disclosure to me eventually became a connect-the-dot, hindsight 20/20, A-ha, light-bulb moment for me. It did not matter how many psychology courses I had taken in either college or university or how many clients I had worked alongside within twenty plus years of crisis-management within social services, or how many paralleled disclosures had been expressed to me, or how many books I read or how many years of research I had personally and professionally undertaken – it took my becoming a Mum, a parent myself to piece it altogether and for me to FINALLY achieve this precision-based clarity and awareness I had been zapped with in that moment of mentally, emotionally, psychologically, and spiritually piecing it together and it making sense to me.

Unbeknownst to my Mum, she had unknowingly and unintentionally gifted me. All the years of hurt, personalization, rejection, alienation, emotional cruelty, abandonment, criticism, grief and loss, for which I had internally struggled with, quite rapidly began to dissipate from me. I did not own it anymore. I was not hanging on to the unspoken words that were never intended to come to me, to put all of this into perspective for me from the very person who I was hoping to hear it from. I saw it and recognized it for the most impossible and unrealistic expectation it was, for which I held and thought I wanted and needed to receive from her. She wasn't capable of this. She was not a-tune or connected to any of it. A disconnected person cannot connect the dots if they are unwilling, unaware or incapable of doing so. I got it. I got my epiphany! I felt as though I had just undergone a spiritual crucifixion, a physical detoxification, and a mental emancipation. I felt completely absolved of it all. Any residual shame, guilt or anguish I may have subconsciously still clung to – evaporated and I had the gift of my baby and the gift of my Mum's disclosure to thank for this. I was no longer conjoined to her in this destructive, counter-intuitive story. The book was closed.

LIVING FEARLESSLY DOWNLOAD

Who am I to determine another person's reality? Who am I to understand the pull, the weight or the gravity of another person's pain or inner conflict? Who am I to assess whether someone is or has chosen to rise within their own lives or question to the degree another person has at all done the work on themselves? No matter the relationship, this is not my business, unless someone chooses to make it my business by choosing to elicit my support, my feedback, my guidance, my anything. That is not to suggest that when you see someone suffering that you merely cast a blind eye and do nothing in the way of offering your services, and of course dependent on the actual situation itself – not waiting for an invitation, but immediately responding with stepping up and stepping in. No two people are going to view a situation in the exact same way. No two people are necessarily going to believe the same things or arrive at the same conclusions as far as anything in life is concerned. One can never go wrong if one remains committed to only focusing on becoming the best possible version of oneself. It all starts with self. Everything derives from self. IT IS A CHOICE!

CHAPTER 17

FULL-CIRCLE-CYCLE

Eighteen months later, I was blessed with a beautiful daughter. My lovely son had become a big brother, and both my pregnancy and delivery were thankfully, smooth sailing. The problems post-birth with my second child were thankfully and immediately, detected and diagnosed by the pediatric doctor, and as a result of not only his medical expertise, but because he had encountered this with his own two children. My daughter, almost immediately upon birth was restless, incessantly crying, unable to sleep and unable to nurse. She was diagnosed with reflux, which mimics colic. She was placed on Prevacid for one year and although this helped, I was advised to expect her symptoms and duress to continue for upwards of one year to eighteen months, before fully running its course and normalizing. Regardless of encountering similar challenges as I had with my firstborn, I was as equally determined and adamant that my second child would also be breast-fed. I was somewhat successful in this pursuit however; my milk for my daughter would not be taken by her at my breast given her physical discomfort for being in the position to nurse. We had received a prescription to rent a state of the art, crème-de-la-crème breast pump from the pharmacy for one full year. I was immensely grateful that although we were unable to establish that additional layer of mother-child-bond that results from nursing that she was at the very least able to receive my breast milk, while being fed in the most creative and inventive positions, possible. To say that we were an exhaustive household, for the first initial couple of years of both children's arrivals into this world, would be a complete understatement.

Although, I came to terms with what my Mum and I were and were not, I still wished to provide her with a do-over opportunity to be in the delivery room with us the second time around. Once again, advanced notice of my anticipated due-date had been provided, safely following the first trimester of my pregnancy. The timeline of my daughter's impending arrival conflicted with my Mum and stepfather's wedding anniversary and another vacation they had anticipated scheduling for themselves, which corresponded with the time Tom (my step-father) was planning to book off from work. In-light of almost being on death's doorstep the first time around and my Mum having opted not to be present for the birth of her first grandchild, was I surprised? Yes, a part of me was. In-light of my deeper clarity and understanding for the scope of who my Mum was in relationship to me, and more importantly – who she was in relationship to herself, was I surprised? No, not at all. The turn-around mindset shift was quick on this one, and so I very swiftly diverted my energies, focus, time and attention to the positives in my life and for what I was continually grateful for. And that, which was out of my control, once again intentionally became background noise. I was getting much better at maneuvering and navigating myself no matter what stayed the same and no matter what changed.

For a whole host of reasons, and for others, which factored in long before I officially got married and for some, which had continued and worsened after the birth of both my children – my marriage had very sadly, imploded. Up until recently, and truthfully, not until, I endeavored to write this book and not even that many previously written chapters ago; I received additional clarity on that particular chapter in my life. I was of the belief that I was in the prime of my life when I had met my then soon to be husband, the father to these two beautiful children. I was in the best shape of my life, top of my game in my career, was debt-free, had banked a respectable amount of monies, had earned both my degree and diploma, was financially independent and had been for many years prior to even having met my husband-to-be, had received many fantastic job offers at the same timing of already having decided to follow Mike out-west after he had received an excellent job offer. I had a fantastic professional portfolio, inclusive of many stellar letters of reference graciously written for and about me. I was a self-accomplished woman. I was a go-getter, and I had earned myself a reputable name in my field of work. I was truly proud of myself. I had done much and had come far from initial beginnings in my start to life. I was immersed in the world of personal growth and development long before it ever became a catch phrase, buzz-word or seemingly new wave or trendy – much because of my prior vocation and the necessity to be that way inclined if ever I was going to aspire to be good at what I did or effective or impactful for those I provided service to. I was equally committed to this journey not only for the betterment of my clients, but also for myself personally, mentally and spiritually. I was committed to re-write my own story, to carve out my own happiness, to overcome my own adversity and rise up for myself in life. I intuitively and innately knew that this could only ever be truly possible if birthed out of self-love, self-forgiveness, self-awareness, and the fierce commitment to self-healing.

I will never negate, undermine or minimize to the degree I did do 'the work' for I have never stopped doing 'the work,' nor do I wish to. No matter the pain, or the revelations or the un-earthed truths, I am not wired to be that individual who buries their head in the sand – pretends that things do not exist, or that things have never before occurred or transpired. I don't know how not to talk about meaningful subject matters or hide behind seemingly safe or superficial topics in one-dimensional conversations. I am the person who does initiate tackling things head on. I will dig deep and then I will dig even deeper. I will face the ugliness. Acknowledge the ugliness and find the solutions to overcome the ugliness. I would not know the first thing about what it means to live in denial – to choose to live in denial or turn a blind eye to any perceivable elephant in the room or elephant weighing heavily on my chest.

Having said that, I continue to get exceptionally clearer within myself, and because this is my truth, I am forever committed to doing 'the work.' And so, the more I work on myself, own my own bullshit, look in the mirror first and foremost, question my own thoughts, my own core beliefs, my own values, my own judgments, my own everything – the more I realize to the degree that no matter what point I think I may have reached and obtained within my own journey of self-awareness, personal growth, and development – I am actually only ever a fraction ahead of where I last was in my thinking or believing of what I understood or embraced as self-truth.

Realizing and acknowledging this about myself and declaring it as my current truth– I can now say that one of my most profound revelations noted within this book has come from the process itself of birthing this book. I do not believe my deeper levels of self-insight and self-reflection would have occurred if not for first choosing to write this book by hand before transcribing my first edit onto the computer. One fact I was not even previously aware of until now, is that no matter how great the packaged Lisa may have appeared at the so-called best time of my life and thinking I had mastered myself enough to embark upon marriage, I now know is not true given my deeper level of having peeled back the onion. I was one hundred percent ready to be a great Mum, which is what I am. I was not ready to have been a great partner at the time of my deciding to get married. It no longer matters what I gave to that relationship or what I sacrificed of myself, both personally or professionally, or how 'evolved' I may have perceivably been, even back then or how I upheld and honored my vows within our entire amount of years in partnership together. It does not matter where he fell short, has admitted to falling short or where I fell short or have admitted to falling short - I now know and realize as it pertains to me and me alone – that I am the common denominator in all my relationships, including first and foremost the relationship I have with myself. I was not healed 'enough – I was not absolved 'enough' – I was not mentally free 'enough' to have made that leap of marriage, no matter how much I may still believe I did my best, gave my best, and was my best at that particular time in my life, within that particular relationship. I was absolutely meant to have exactly these two beautiful children and they would not be exactly who they are if not for who exactly I had those children with. Our time and place together was exactly what was meant to be at the exact time for the exact purpose and reason of us having these two exact children as they are. It really is that simple. Hypothetically speaking, even if I had these newfound insights, which I do now – back at the time of my still being married – it may not have been enough to have saved us or to have healed us within our partnership to one another and perhaps I may not have these newfound insights, had I remained in my marriage. One can never say for sure. It is all speculation, but at least I care enough to question it regardless of whether or not it is a moot point. I am grateful for these two children. I am grateful to their father for making that possible and giving me the most important, most cherished gifts of my life. I am grateful that he is a fantastic father and I am grateful for the majority of the time, we have become amicable, healthy, fair, rational, and that most importantly, we are consistently on the same page that our children, and their well-being will always be non-negotiable. I honestly do believe as well, that for where we were both at individually, separate from the marriage itself, that we each did our best with what we had to work with and for whom we each were at the time, to try and make things work. I do not take that away from him, nor do I take that away from myself.

LIVING FEARLESSLY DOWNLOAD

If I am to profess wishing to see a more peaceful, unified, love-filled type of world for my children and my children's children, then it is my responsibility to first create a micro-culture, which fosters, nourishes, and cultivates that which is necessary within myself and within my family home. Endeavoring to create a solid in-house approach first and foremost then allows me the positive space to expand upon the macro levels of culture. The biggest leaps originate from first taking the smallest of steps. The core ingredients essential for harvesting a fruitful life resides within each of us. Leading a prosperous, successful and abundant life is essentially dependent upon one's own mindset. How one thinks sets the tone and stage for how one executes, navigates and maneuvers in life. When one views themselves as a worthy investment and makes daily deposits into self – this becomes a win-win recipe for each individual person, their family, their community and ultimately – for all of humanity. If each of us elevated to assume personal ownership, responsibility and accountability for our own thoughts, beliefs, choices, actions and decisions – what a phenomenal shift we would all stand to benefit from. If each of us was equally prepared and committed to asking ourselves, "Do I wish to be solution-focused or problem-saturated?" – what a legacy this generation could leave behind for our children and our grandchildren to deservingly inherit. The solution is internal not external. IT IS A CHOICE!

CHAPTER 18

THE LAST TIME

When the children and I had transplanted ourselves in 2011 back to the town I had been born and raised in, this as a result of tough decisions needing to be made during one of the darkest times in my life – I did my best – we all did our best to slowly move forward, putting one foot in front of the other, and not knowing how this was all going to unfold – for him, for me or for either of the children. There was no manual for marriage, or for parenthood, let alone for divorce. My mindset kicked into high gear with knowing I needed to provide, the now three of us, with a solid infrastructure of support. Because we had decided to keep all of our problems to ourselves, sparing our families the details of the why's or the how's of how we had gotten 'here' – our move from Alberta back to Ontario had inevitably created misunderstanding on both sides of the family, as to what our reason for returning home to be truly indicative of. It had naturally been presumed that our return home was founded on the fact that we now had children and therefore, wished to have our children raised with family close by. There was of course truth to that, but the picture of what family now looked like was very much changing from the previously intact nuclear constellation picture everyone else had primarily been working with.

I had the daunting task of returning to Dundas sans children to go house hunting with a real-estate agent I had secured, while still living in Alberta. Our home out-west had already sold with a fast approaching closing/move out date looming over us, coupled with the children's father having already secured a start date for his new career position in Madagascar, Africa for a three year contract – six weeks out, ten days back here with the children in Ontario, times three years. It was of course, an extremely stressful and highly emotional time in all of our lives and with a rapid succession of major life transitions all occurring simultaneously. We were both respectful and on the same page with the agreement, until we knew for absolute certain that this was not just a temporary separation, but in fact a permanent departure of ways bearing of course in mind, the reality that our children would forever keep us joined and connected to one another – that we would keep these most recent developments to ourselves. My former in-laws were in the know as we required tangible support in the packing up of our house and the house showings in Alberta given we had two small children to consider with the logistics of all that goes into the selling of a home. We needed and very much appreciated the help, although it being a tumultuous time for all.

Given that this newfound reality was a mountainous one to have to adjust and transition into, I was finding it increasingly unbearable to wear the mask with others and maintain the façade that the four of us were embarking upon this chapter in our lives under the presumed guise that all was bliss and joy. One day, I finally just came out and asked Mike to copy everyone on an email, detailing the facts of what our present and impending circumstances were and would be. The record needed to be set straight. The truth needed to be shared so we could authentically begin to heal and adapt.

At the time of the email being circulated, my Mum was in England visiting her own Mum – my Grandma. My step-father (had communicat-

ed) the contents of my email to my Mum, while she had been abroad.
I was openly perturbed about that. One because any precious time able
to be spent between my Grandma and my Mum was sacred, given their
mutual health issues and concerns, not to mention my Grandma's age
and geographical distance and her own stressors related to having had
one daughter already pass on, due to metastatic breast cancer and now her
only other surviving (adult) child, also having the same aggressive form
of disease. Whatever time they were both additionally afforded with one
another, I believe should have been respected and protected without the
shockingly sad news affecting or adversely impacting the quality of their
limited time together.

Upon receiving the update of MY life, my Mum in-turn divulged that
same information to my Grandma. Mike and I had been in agreement of
not wishing to share our news with either of our grandmothers. I was ex-
pressive with both my Mum and stepfather over the telephone, once my
Mum had returned home from England, of my hurt for how this very intimate and dark chapter in my life was thoughtlessly being discussed and
handled. Those copied on the email were the only ones we wished to have
aware of our circumstances. Had I thought for a second that my Mum
(who I knew would not have access to email, while abroad in the U.K.)
would have been told during her travels, we would not have included my
Mum or my stepfather in the group email.

My expressed disappointment and hurt for how this all played out on
the communication front was met with defensiveness, dismissiveness and
even offense. This particular incident only served to heighten and magnify every other colossal event having transpired in my life, with respect to
the repeated historical patterns of having been invalidated, unacknowl-
edged and even swept under the rug and somehow (without surprise)
turned around on me as though things having been perpetrated upon me

or my reactions to such injustices were completely unwarranted and unfounded. I became very mindful of how this culmination and accumulation of consistently re-visiting this twilight zone of perpetual surrealness, had truly worn me out. It was too much. Nothing ever seemed to change – the dynamics, the patterns, the behaviors, - the constant rut of it all. It was all unhealthily predictable and counter-intuitive. It did not matter the depth of the crisis, nor the excitement of the milestone – the outcome was always the same.

As a result of this broken story, always finding a way or an opportunity to re-tell itself by rearing its ugly head – no matter the efforts I valiantly made to put distance between myself and all of it – all of them – the only way for me to navigate away from this same shit, different day, broken record, was to end the discussion with the statement, "Let's agree to disagree and leave it there. I do not wish to talk about this anymore, please." Before hanging up the phone, it was reiterated, once again, that they were planning to make the road-trip out to the children and I here in Dundas, with the said intention of offering the three of us their support during what they identified as an emotionally tough time in our lives. The children who because of their young ages could not quite recall who Grandma and Grandpa Reid were – were excited nonetheless, to learn that we were having members of our family come to stay with us in our home. We all welcomed the additional voices, faces and quite simply, we were eager for the mere distraction and interruption from our daily scheduled routines. I also was grateful for the anticipated extra pair of hands to play, to feed, maybe even change a diaper as flying solo for six weeks at a time until their Dad returned from Madagascar, left me feeling depleted and robotic at times.

My Mum and Tom pulled up in the driveway a couple of hours before the munchkins were to go to bed for the evening. The children were excited and were immediately receptive to sitting on laps, giving and receiving hugs and kisses and were overjoyed to open up some lovely presents given to them from their Grandparents. My Mum and Tom rhymed off some ideas they had previously come up with on their own for possible daily excursions and activities we could all partake in together, during their four or five day stay with us. The Butterfly Conservatory specifically mentioned, had both the children eager and excited. Before putting the children to bed, they were both made aware that their other set of Grandparents, Mike's parents, had been graciously agreeable to come by the house the next day to take the munchkins out for the better part of the late morning and early afternoon so as to give my Mum, Tom and I the opportunity as three adults to talk face-to-face for the first time since news broke of Mike and I separating and proceeding with legally un-coupling.

I can only speak for myself, but the next day of seeing all 'the parents' congregated in my kitchen and being in the presence of one another for the first time since the day Mike and I had gotten married in Virginia in 2007 – now fast forward to 2012 – as cordial, and pleasant. And as kind as they all were toward one another, I could naturally detect a layer of expectant awkwardness and discomfort for everyone and understandably so. The three of us kissed and hugged the munchkins goodbye – promising to see them soon and wishing them a fun day with Grandma and Papa. The munchkins had snuck into their goodbyes, the reminder of The Butterfly Conservatory and given their mentioning it with lit up faces, it was clear to everyone, how happy they were to have family visiting and outings to look forward to. It truly warmed my heart to see my children laughing and smiling and excited to have things to look forward to, especially during such heavy-hearted times.

What none of us could have known in that moment of saying goodbye and going our separate ways for the afternoon, is that this would be the last time they would ever again see Grandma and Grandpa Reid and sadly, there would be no group family outing to The Butterfly Conservatory or anywhere else, which was what had been voluntarily promised to the two of them.

I hopped into their vehicle and out of my driveway we reversed – off to a quaint little restaurant called, The Bean Bar in Westdale, Hamilton – about ten minutes up the road from where I live. Conversation was seemingly light and comfortable with one another for the quick drive it took, before arriving at our destination. We decided upon the window table to the immediate right of the restaurants entrance. The restaurant itself is a small, intimate venue with a great vibe and for all the times I had previously been there, not unlike on this particular occasion, it was always filled with a good mix of professionals, university students and also known as a great place to frequent if out on a date.

Mum and Tom sat with their backs facing the window of the restaurant, while I sat directly across from the two of them. The waiter had kindly introduced himself, while pouring our glasses full with water, offering us menus and asking if we'd like to start with a beverage. While perusing the menus and awaiting our drinks, Tom initiated the conversation opener, "I still can't get over the shock of opening up your email." My first thought to myself, "You've got to be kidding me." I instantly began talking myself down, before I ventured to open my mouth. Knowing my history with them, I was very methodical and selective in the choosing of my words that would follow. The last thing I wanted to see happen, especially during this already raw and fragile state I was in and knowing how happy the children were to have them both visiting us, was a blow out. I purposely exercised constraint. I responded with only calmness and diplomacy when the next words to follow were mine.

"Well, as you know based on how this subject was last left between us on the phone and my not wishing to further discuss the email aspect specifically, and ending the conversation with saying, 'Let's agree to dis-agree' I would not have initiated bringing this back up again but given that you have and we are now sitting face to face with one another – all I will say on the subject, again – is that I was hurt with how a very private and painful matter to me was shared in the manner in which it was and that Grandma was told. I only wanted to be heard by you and to have my feelings validated by you even if we share a different point of view. That's it. That was all I was trying to express to you both over the phone."

Things immediately digressed and went completely south (both lit-erally and figuratively) from that moment forward. The three of us were back on the landmine, doing our usual jig. I felt so utterly sorry for our poor, un-suspecting, waiter. From the point of delivering us our drinks, to his first check-in to see if we were ready to place our orders, he visibly sensed right away that something nasty was going down at our table as did a few of the other patrons sitting closest to our table. Somehow we went from me saying what I said, to my Mum dropping f-bombs, calling me a Martyr, to her then storming straight out of the restaurant. Happy Times! Go-Team! Tom and I knew she was headed to the neighboring card shop as she had already indicated her wanting to go there after lunch.

Tom looked at me, pitching to me how my Mum's current cancer-cock-tail regimen had her more agitated and short-tempered than usual. He elaborated by saying that if my Mum perceived any outward slight, hos-tility or ill feelings toward her that she would not comfortably put herself in the position of staying with myself and the children at my home. This was followed up with him encouraging me to go chase her down – to apologize – to make amends – to basically smooth it over with her.

Another 'what the hell' thought to self. Was he for real? He was the one who opened up the can of worms we had agreed to keep shut, given how heated the subject matter had escalated to in the first place. For the children's sake and for my already having reached my threshold for what I could emotionally and mentally withstand and for my own self-preservation, the last thing consciously or subconsciously I would ever initiate or invite under my own present circumstances, was world war III – especially with these two. I did not have it in me, had already beyond maxed out the quota for this needless drama and toxicity in one possible lifetime. My nerves and my emotions were already dangling by a thread. I was in need of help. I was in need of support. I was in need of calm and quiet. I was starving for peace in my life. I was only asking people to meet me half way with respect to boundaries and everyone grasping the bigger picture – for the children first and foremost. Why was it so impossible for people to rise? To want to choose to rise up? No matter my history with the two of them, I had become an expert at picking my battles. I had mentally and emotionally already been doing the inner work (as I always have) in preparation for their arrival to my home. Everything from my perspective was prefaced with only gratitude, relief and excitement for their visit because I knew exactly how I was feeling, struggling and desperately welcomed the distraction, the interaction, the company. I welcomed and embraced that for myself and especially for my deserving children. Sabotage was nowhere on the radar. Four days of anticipated help and support, four days of an extra pair of hands – was a gift to me. I knew better and not just with them – never to kick a gift-horse in the mouth. This would be almost comical if not for my innocent children who were in the throes and on the cusp of becoming collateral damage in all of this – needlessly and selfishly.

Tom and I both exited the restaurant – he indicating to me that he wanted to talk to my Mum first, before figuring out the next course of action. Originally, the plan was for the three of us to have a lovely meal together, followed up by a trip over to the Chapter's bookstore in Ancaster, for the purpose of my wanting to purchase an additional belated Mother's Day Gift for my Mum – something I myself had, which she had expressed liking and interested in getting for herself – a particular fragrance product. As far as I knew, it could only be found at Chapter's so I had suggested we pop over so I could pick up a bottle for her. It made me happy to know that I could gift her with something she not only liked and personally wanted, but in this case, something she could wear and hopefully be reminded of me every time she smelt the scent, and long after our visit had come to an end. The days of buying Mother/ Daughter Statues were over for me so this was a good compromise for me, personally. The eternal optimist in me had envisioned her thinking of me every time she would apply it to herself or anytime she might receive a compliment when she wore it – maybe mentioning that her daughter in Canada had given it to her. Me always hallucinating and imagining a happier, more positive outcome and renewed beginnings for the two of us and our relationship.

When body language suggested it was safe and appropriately timed for me to physically approach, both my Mum and Tom, who at this point were standing about ten feet away from me, on the sidewalk and around the corner from the restaurant – I, like a child, looked to them for direction as to what the next move was to be. I hesitated to speak and thought it completely wise on my part to take my cue from them. When I was told we were leaving – I more than half expected to hear this from them (given the amount of embarrassment we had brought upon ourselves inside the restaurant). I was more than relieved as you might well imagine.

Back in the vehicle we went. When it became clear to me that we were not diverging left into the turning lane – the direction we needed to take off Main Street to go to Ancaster to go to where Chapter's was located, it was then I started to feel that sinking feeling in the pit of my stomach and the immediate lump that comes out of nowhere and lands smack dab in the middle of your throat.

"Where are we going? Ancaster is back that way. We missed the left hand turn." Now we were descending down the big hill that connects Hamilton to Dundas – now by-passing the University Plaza on the left hand side, which is synonymous of my childhood and everyone else's too, who grew up in Dundas. Instant flashbacks sprung to mind of all the times my Mum and I frequented the Plaza, especially the Coles Book-store, which was our favorite place to hang out in and peruse the aisles – the same place unbeknownst to either my Mum or myself (at the time) of where I would host my own book signings – a milestone my Mum would never come to know or to partake in. "Where are we going?" I asked.

My Mum spoke up. "We're going back to your house, getting our belongings, and then we are leaving."

"What about the kids – they're not even due back at the house for another couple of hours. How are you going to explain to them the reason you are leaving? What about The Butterfly Conservatory – what about everything else you promised them they had to look forward to? You've not even spent one full day with them doing anything or going anywhere. Please do not do this to them. Please don't disappoint them like this – they have been through far too much already. They are excited and happy to have you with us. Please let's not put them in the middle of our issues. Please just drop me off and at least think about it – maybe go for a drive – maybe stay in a hotel here, locally if you don't feel comfortable being around me or in my house. I trust you with the children. I don't have to go with you on any of the outings you promised the children. I can stay behind. Please do not do this!" I pleaded. I was bawling by this point, negotiating, compromising, bartering and pleading. I could not believe the degree we had now sunk to. I expected this where I was concerned, but I honestly in my heart-of-hearts, believed it would be a different story where my own children – her grandchildren, were concerned.

The fact that her daughter was going through a divorce, a life-altering hardship for which she had first-hand experience with herself, and she was just going to bail like this. She knew the pain I was in – she had lived it herself. I was in the exact same predicament she was also in once-upon-a-time. Her pain was so unbearable and debilitating that she had even seriously considered and almost followed through on overdosing herself and her own two children. She was going to end it for all of us.

When I realized there was no reasoning with her or persuading her to re-consider or to change her mind at all no matter my valiant efforts to compromise to negotiate to rationalize – to shed light and put into perspective how devastated and confused her two innocent grandchildren were going to be left feeling, I lost my shit.

"You know if you do this, Mum, you know if you leave me and the munchkins like this, we will never, ever, see each other again and that is on you and both of us fully know that you have terminal, metastatic, aggressive cancer. You know that this will be on you – not me – you've made the decision for everyone involved. It is YOU who is turning your back on these children and your family and that is with you, knowing it is the lowest time in our lives. These are YOUR grandchildren. Your time with them is already limited and short-changed because of geographics, and because of your cancer. It will be YOU who has to live with the knowledge that YOU broke my children's hearts and thank you very much for putting me in this position of having to face Mike's parents and the kids and having to explain to a four and a one and a half year old where the hell Grandma and Grandpa Reid have disappeared to and why. How do I explain this to them when I cannot even begin to understand it myself, at all, on any level? I'm going through hell Mum and you're going to dump this on me and leave me to be the one to have to hurt and disappoint my children when we have had plenty of that already? Can you not at the very least make up an excuse of why you have to return home to the States and at least give them a hug and a kiss goodbye first? They deserve that, Mum. This isn't about you or me, it's about them. Please don't do this. Please don't go out like this.

"We're going, Lisa," was all she would say to me. We pulled into my driveway. I told her the door to the house was un-locked– told her to get her shit and told her to get out of my house and out of my life once and for all. Told Tom to reverse out of the driveway so I could fly out of there in my own parked-in vehicle. I needed to collect myself and figure out a story that would somewhat wash with two toddlers whose lives had already been turned upside down. I wanted and needed to get out of there ASAP before seeing my Mum exit my house and have to watch the two of them drive down my street for the last time, and out of our lives forever.

LIVING FEARLESSLY DOWNLOAD

Rather than becoming consumed with negative energies, resentments and things I could not control, I chose to transform all those energies into love and channeled it full-throttle into the parenting and loving of my two beautiful children. I was not going to distract myself with the mootness of what I did not understand or comprehend with our mother/daughter relationship - instead, I was going to forever choose to pour my everything, that which truly mattered, and that which is pure, and kind and loving into my children. No matter my own current or future issues or challenges I may have with either one of them as they get older – them seeing the back of me or questioning my love for them will never make it to that list. I could not change, control or alter what I deeply wanted from my own mother, but I could take responsibility and assume ownership for the type of parent I chose to be to my own children. They deserved to have me present for them not checked out because of her. They came first – ahead of everyone and everything – always. IT IS A CHOICE!

CHAPTER 19

THE PHONE CALL

That was the last time I ever saw or spoke to my Mum. She passed away two years later with a parting message intended for me and promised by my step-father to her, to relay to me when he would have to place the telephone call, informing me of my Mum's passing.

10:30pm – June 27, 2014

"Lisa, its Tom. Your Mum died at 8:30pm earlier tonight in hospice. She made me promise to tell you something she said in one of her last most lucid moments, which she asked that I communicate to you after she passed away. Your Mum wanted me to tell you that she forgives you and that she had prayed to Jesus Christ to ask him to forgive you, too."

THE BEGINNING

EPILOGUE

I believe it our inherent birthright to thrive and flourish in this fascinating miracle we call LIFE. I quite confidently and deservingly believe I have earned the right to declare myself a 'SPIRITUAL WARRIOR,' not un-like many of you here who have very graciously taken the time to read my story, and of whom my story may personally resonate with on some level and in some regard.

The intention of my book was not at all to speak-ill of anyone or to cast others, namely my Mum, in a negative light. My Mum had a plethora of terrific qualities and was loved, and admired by many. My Mum positively touched and impacted many people who crossed paths with her throughout her lifetime and many as a result of their kinship to her through the personal journey of Cancer. She was a beacon of light and hope for many who were equally afflicted by the disease.

In my earlier years, I found myself envious of anyone on the receiving end of my Mum's attentiveness, her genuine concern and who were the recipient of her outstretched hands eagerly, lovingly, and willingly wishing to prop others up and walk alongside them in their own personal journey. For those who received the gift of her advocacy, her un-conditional support, compassionate and empathetic shoulder to cry on, I am genuinely happy for you that you had each other to triumph, rally, and cheer one another on. I begrudge no one the unique and special bond you may have shared in with my Mum.

Although, I was not intended to have the mother-daughter closeness and so-called in-destructible bond, I had always craved and longed for and although I never received traditional closure following my Mum's passing, such as, customary details or an invitation to attend her service, nor was I allowed to know of the many weeks she had resided in palliative care, prior to her eventual passing, and although it was imperative to my Mum that her last expressed words and sentiments for me, echo the same histrionic patterns of passive-aggressiveness and emotional cruelty as when she was alive – in –spite of her last message wanting or needing to be conveyed to me being exactly as she chose it to be, rather than one, which conversely spoke to LOVE – loving me, I LOVE YOU, I am sorry, I am proud of you, be happy, hope you can or will forgive me (meaning her) I love my grandchildren – any of those expressed sentiments that most dying mothers would choose to impart as their last words to their children either directly or indirectly – it crystallized everything for me.

In fact, what she may never realize is that she gave me the greatest gift with her parting message to me being exactly as it was. As a mother myself to both a son and a daughter, I will never, ever be able to conceive of or fathom this type of parent-child relationship or dynamic. However, like everything else in my life that I may not have necessarily understood or received adequate closure on, I have instead, as I have cited throughout the entirety of my book, chosen to focus on the gifts, the lessons, the ways in which I can turn darkness into brightness and not only for myself but for the collective. I believe this is my purpose. I believe this to be my personal, Universal-Calling in life.

Not only have I used my own life experiences within my journey to pay-it-forward and consistently be of service-to-others, but I have also used my transferable skills from my previous vocation in social services by incorporating my personal MISSION of serving others, into my current vocation and life's passions of being an author, a radio and TV show host, a podcaster, a speaker, mentor, and life coach, and using all of my various platforms (as a vehicle) to impart my message of Living Fearlessly to others. I choose to stand for empowering the collective, to assist others in getting un-stuck in their own lives, to help others reclaim and reinvent themselves, by also being the example myself, of how to fear less and to live more by turning pain into passions, which I believe, is how one un-leashes their Purpose.

I am a staunch believer that self-empowerment, self-love, self-for-giveness, self-awareness and self-belief are vital and essential to learning how to re-write the story in one's own life. To completely de-program and de-construct all the limiting and false beliefs, which disallows one to operate at their highest vibrational level, to truly love one's own life, to manifest true abundance in one's own life and to appreciate the gift and miracle, which life truly is.

I have immense heartfelt gratitude for my Mum, for being much of the reason, foundation and catalyst in my evolution of self, and in my overall life journey. Without everything having transpired exactly as it did, I may not be exactly as I am today, doing exactly what I am doing, which I am only too proud, humbled and honored to be a part of with those I am mutually and equally aligned with – those I refer to as 'my' TRIBE. Had it not been for my life experiences, I may not have grown or evolved into being a person who is impassioned to serve others. I may not be as compassionate, caring, kind, concerned, connected or plugged-in to the degree I aspire to be every single day I am afforded additional time and privilege to breathe and to thrive on this planet.

My Last Word's To You Mum:

Dearest Mum,

Thank you for giving birth to me, Mum. Thank you for providing me with this beautiful gift of life. I appreciate you for being so instrumental in my journey and for being much of the driving force and underlying reason behind my knowing, with every fiber of my being, what my exact purpose is here on earth. Please know I do have fond memories of us and I reflect upon them often. I will never harbor resentment toward you, as to do so would be counter-intuitive and would only serve to further shackle myself to the past of things I cannot reverse, cannot change and cannot undo. I do not pretend to have control over anything, other than my own attitude, my own mindset, and my own choices. For the ways I am sure I have hurt you, I apologize. For the ways you have hurt me, I forgive you. For all that happened to you in your lifetime which brought you pain and suffering – please know the child in me hugs and loves the child in you. I know you love me, Mum. Please know that I know that. Please know that I too, love you. Wherever you are, Mum - please know that I forever send you all my love, well-wishes, and eternal blessings. Maybe we get it right next time, okay?

Love and Light to you, Mum ~

Lisa

CPSIA information can be obtained
at www.ICGtesting.com
Printed in the USA
BVHW04s1428241018
531112BV00015B/266/P

9 781628 655865